— WASHINGTON —

FOOD ARTISANS

WASHINGTON

FOOD ARTISANS

Farm Stories and Chef Recipes

LEORA Y. BLOOM

Photographs by Clare Barboza

SASQUATCH BOOKS
SEATTLE

To the farmers, foragers, and fishermen of Washington, who keep us all so well fed.

Printed in China

Published by Sasquatch Books
17 16 15 14 13 12   9 8 7 6 5 4 3 2 1

Cover design: Anna Goldstein
Cover photographs: Clare Barboza
Interior design and composition: Anna Goldstein
Interior photographs: Clare Barboza, Turnbow Flat Farms (pages 70 and 73), and Rachelle Longé (lobster mushroom and blackberries on page 140)

Library of Congress Cataloging-in-Publication Data is available.

ISBN-13: 978-1-57061-660-0
ISBN-10: 1-57061-660-4

Sasquatch Books
1904 Third Avenue, Suite 710
Seattle, WA 98101
(206) 467-4300
www.sasquatchbooks.com
custserv@sasquatchbooks.com

CONTENTS

RECIPES BY COURSE

ACKNOWLEDGMENTS

I never could have written this book without the generosity of all these incredible food artisans. They took time out of their busy lives to patiently explain what they do and how they do it, and they graciously allowed me to ask all sorts of personal questions in order to better understand *why* they do it. More than anything, I hope they are happy with the end result. They are (in order by chapter): Don Hilario Alvarez, Eddie Alvarez, Billy Allstot, Brent Olsen, Stephen Robins, Brooke Lucy, Beverly Phillips, Steve Phillips, Kurt Timmermeister, Mary MacDonald, Duncan MacDonald, Pete Knutson, Bill Whitbeck, James Hall, Gretchen Hoyt, Jerry Pipitone, Stina Booth, Donna Westom, Roy Nettlebeck, Rick Middleton, and John Bookwalter.

Having worked in restaurant kitchens, I know exactly how busy chefs are. Never very comfortable asking for favors, I was terrified by the process of gathering all this inside information. But my fears were all for naught. As soon as I explained what the project was about, all of the chefs helped me in so many ways: some offered recipes; some met with me and explained why they are so loyal to local producers; some gave me lists of producers to consider and other chefs to contact. All were kind and helped make this book a joy to work on. They are: Brittany Bardeleben, Ericka Burke, Dana Cree, Danielle Custer, Kelly Daly, Matt Dillon, Tom Douglas, James Drohman, Lisa Dupar, Charlie Durham, Heather Earnhardt, Jason Franey, Mark Fuller, Chester Gerl, Dylan Giordan, Daisley Gordon, John Gunnar, Craig Hetherington, Maria Hines, John Howie, Anson Klock, Jenny Klock, Robin Leventhal, Vuong Loc, Keith Luce, Leslie Mackie, Amy McCray, Jeremy McLachlan, Bobby Moore, Walter Pisano, Nick Pitsilionis, Thierry Rathureau, Angie Roberts, Adria Shimada, Adam Stevenson, Ethan Stowell, Jason Stratton, Jack Strong, John Sundstrom, Sabrina Tinsley, Todd Torgerson, Jerry Traunfeld, Andrew Wilson, Jason Wilson, Jeffrey Wilson, and Ron Zimmerman. In particular, Chef Charlie Durham not only contributed recipes, he also helped me test recipes.

Chris Curtis, director of the Neighborhood Farmers Market Alliance in Seattle, got me off to a great start by helping me grasp all the different ways in which we benefit by buying directly from producers, and by introducing me to a number of "her" fabulous farmers. Jamie Peha, principal of Peha Promotions and former marketing director for the Washington State Wine Commission, helped me understand what a challenge it would be to choose just two wineries to represent the hundreds of fine ones we have in Washington. She shared the stories of how many of them came to be, and I'm pretty sure there's another book in there. . . .

Besides talking to strangers, the part of this project that scared me the most was the massive amount of transcribing that was needed in order for me to write accurate profiles. Sumedh Kanetkar taught me how to ready my sound files and upload them to Amazon's

Mechanical Turk, which saved the day, mostly by connecting me with Sherry Segers in Columbus, Ohio. She transcribed countless hours of conversation, and did most of it in the middle of the night.

Netter Hansen read every bit of this book, most of it more than once, and her suggestions along the way made every piece of it stronger. Robin Martin, Sherri Wolson, Linda McElroy, and Katie McCann tested recipes for me and provided helpful notes to ensure the success of every recipe in this book. Linda also read and copyedited for me—even when she was on vacation! Dawn Thomas, Kimberley Slobodian, and Diane de Ryss read the manuscript and so clearly heard my message; they were the ones who gave me the confidence to finally hit "Send." Robin Martin not only managed to test almost every recipe in this book (many of them more than once), she also read the book in its entirety, all while running after and raising three small children. In her spare time she acted as my head cheerleader and primary snack provider.

Susan Roxborough first suggested that I pitch an idea to her at Sasquatch Books, and then had enough faith in me to champion the book. Managing editor Rachelle Longé polished my manuscript until it shined, with help from eagle-eyed copy editors Kim Runciman and Lisa Gordanier. Susan also introduced me to Clare Barboza, whose beautiful photographs help bring these artisans, their food, and their stunning locales to life. And then designer Anna Goldstein put it all together in such a beautiful way, I couldn't be more proud of the final result.

My mother-in-law, Marlene Bloom, not only read everything I sent her, but she asked for more. She and my father-in-law, Rudy Bloom, sent me related reading material from Toronto whenever they came across it. There are few things that make a daughter-in-law happier than knowing her parents-in-law are proud of her.

My parents, Ruth Ann and Errol Ger, have been telling me for at least 25 years that I should and could write a book. They read every piece of this one as I wrote and rewrote it—according to them, it was perfect when I started and even better now. If I can do for my children even half of what they've done for me, I'll consider myself a success.

My husband, Paul Bloom, held my hand every step of the way. He accompanied me on my first interviewing trip so that I wouldn't have to travel alone, and hunted for wi-fi while I learned about growing apples and grains. When I got brave enough to travel by myself, he took care of our three kids single-handedly—and that is not easy. He believed right from the start that I could write this book, and even though it'll have to sell a few hundred thousand copies to cover the cost of the babysitters, he's always made me feel like it was a great idea and an excellent investment. While their friends ate macaroni and cheese, my children—Harry, Leah, and Sadie—ate truffles, chicken liver pâté, morels, and curried lentils, mostly without complaining. When one of my three-year-olds looked at her plate and announced, "Oh, good! I love chanterelles," it made my heart full.

INTRODUCTION

In the Beginning

In August 2009, just as I was preparing to write this book, The Herbfarm Restaurant in Woodinville presented a "100-Mile Dinner" series. It sounded like the perfect way to celebrate the beginning of this project, and in fact, that dinner turned out to be an edible version of this book: fabulous raw ingredients from fascinating producers crafted with a reverent touch into a truly memorable meal.

The restaurant had begun work on the series a year earlier when owner Ron Zimmerman threw out a challenge to his kitchen: "What if we create a dinner where every ingredient—plant, animal, mineral, liquid—comes from no more than 100 miles from the table?"

His chefs and kitchen staff embraced the concept with a passion that surprised even Zimmerman, who constantly motivates his staff to "truly know the local stuff" so that there's little need for them to reach very far for ingredients.

Explains Zimmerman, "If you're fortunate enough to live in a place like the Northwest, where you can grow virtually everything at some point during the year, then you can have an amazing diet of local things that have extraordinary flavors, and you can feel really connected to where you live."

While The Herbfarm gathered its foodstuffs from no farther than 100 miles, I had all of the great state of Washington to draw from when I went looking for food artisans to interview. With an area of more than 70,000 square miles, elevations from sea level to the top of Mount Rainier at 14,410 feet, microclimates ranging from the lush rainforest in the West that gets as much as 170 inches of rain a year, to the desert around the Tri-Cities that averages less than 8 inches, the variety of products that flourish here is truly astounding. Along the way, I found out than when you start looking more closely at your food, you also discover the people and the stories behind the food. And as Zimmerman pointed out during the dinner, "People are engaged by stories."

With thousands of Washington artisans to choose from, deciding whose story to tell proved a difficult task. Everyone has a story worth telling, and each one could fill a book. In the end, I chose a cross-section of people whose outstanding products are available in the Seattle area as well as in other locales around the state where consumers are seeking high-quality local products.

As I criss-crossed the state to meet everyone, I was stopped in my tracks by the stunning beauty of Washington's rainforests, alpine peaks, desert flatlands, gurgling rivers, and rolling hillsides of orchards, grains, and vines. Now when I stand at my local farmers market, peering into crates of crisp chard, barrels of glowing plums, and ice chests of oysters, I am reminded not only of the awe-inspiring vistas of Washington, but also the fascinating stories of the paths these producers took to feed me, and the effort and dedication they put into their products.

Connections

Just as a painting means so much more to us if we meet the artist, and a restaurant meal becomes more memorable when we meet the chef, so knowing the person who cared for our food and brought it to us gives it value far beyond what we pay for it. Face-to-face interactions are an added bonus in this age of technological go-betweens—they create a stronger sense of community, and that's a very real benefit of buying from local farmers, fishermen, ranchers, and foragers. I've learned that the simple act of buying food from a local producer not only creates personal pleasure and connections, but can have tremendous economic impact as well. So many of the farmers I talked to explained with passion that, yes, they get a better price for their products when they sell directly to their customers—but also that the money they bring home supports local businesses, which in turn improves the financial health of nearby communities.

The producers featured here stand behind their products—literally. Stina Booth and her husband, John Richardson, take turns driving their truck across the Cascades to bring their apples and pears to Seattle so that someone is always at home taking care of the trees. Beverly and Steve Phillips don't take vacations because the health and happiness of their goats is so important to them, they can't imagine leaving them even overnight. Donna Westom has been foraging in many of the same spots all her life, so she's acutely aware of how healthy the environment needs to be to produce wild foods, and she's adamant about doing what she can to maintain it.

Food That Inspires

Back in the mid-'90s, I moved from Washington, DC, to San Francisco to work in the pastry kitchen of a fine dining restaurant near the Ferry Building downtown. Cameron Ryan, the pastry chef I worked for, was truly inspired by her ingredients, and she taught me to respect and honor them as well as the farmers who grew them. Every Saturday she'd leave me a shopping list—but her note at the top said to "just get whatever was best" at the market. I'd take a hand truck downstairs to the Ferry Plaza and spend the best hour of my week at the farmers market there. I was new to the city, but I felt part of the community when Moses the Egg Man or Farmer Al from Frog Hollow Farm greeted me. Once everything was back at the restaurant, Cameron adapted the menu to showcase the gorgeous ingredients I'd found.

When I moved to the Seattle area to open my own bakery, Pike Place Market was the only year-round farmers market here. But today there are many—in Seattle, across Washington, and across the country. And now I know that once you have met the producers, the way you look at your food changes. When I see a tomato sitting in my kitchen, I think of all the time, effort, experience, and passion that Billy Allstot put into it, and there's absolutely no way I'd ever leave it to spoil on the counter. It's too delicious and too precious. And herein lay the challenge for the chefs who so kindly contributed recipes to this book: When an ingredient is fantastic, you don't really have to do much to it—but how interesting is a recipe that says, "1 carrot. Eat."?

Fortunately, just as we are lucky to have a seemingly endless supply of magnificent local food, we are also blessed with myriad brilliant chefs here in Washington. The chefs I approached already understood the incredible, positive ramifications of "buying local." They responded enthusiastically to the project and generously contributed recipes. They had already searched far and wide for the finest ingredients for their restaurants; they'd found them right here in Washington, and they wanted to help spread the word. Some of these recipes are simple, others are more complicated, but every single one of them is not only worth making, but is truly memorable. And no matter the season, there's a recipe here for something you can get from Washington.

"Buy Local"

Sixty years ago, buying food from local sources was our only option, and we're just now realizing how good we used to have it. The shorter the distance our food has to travel, the fresher we get it; and the fresher we get it, the better it tastes and the more likely we are to buy it again. Farmland is a finite natural resource. Simple economics dictate that once land has been rezoned from farmland to residential or commercial, it doesn't ever change back. Open spaces, including farmland, are not only important because they're beautiful and part of what makes Washington special, but also because they keep our air and water clean. Buying local foods is the best way to ensure the preservation of Washington farmland and other open spaces.

Today it is not unusual to find food in our supermarkets that has traveled from the other side of the world. It was harvested days, weeks, even months before, and has been handled by untold numbers of people before it finds its way to us. It has been developed, above all else, to survive the trip intact. In other words, it's more important that a piece of fruit looks good than tastes good. The farmer who grew it often earns only a tiny percentage of our purchase price, and the farther away the product was raised, the farther away we send our money. We're so removed from the source that it's nearly impossible to know who benefits (or suffers) as a result.

I still love ingredients from far-flung places, like Meyer lemons, chocolate, coffee, and vanilla beans, and I will continue to buy them. But the more we buy from local producers, the better our local economy, the healthier our environment, the tastier and more nutritious our meals. When chefs like the ones in this book embrace local food producers, they make quite an impact. But we as individuals can, too. When I'm shopping for food, I look first for the products of local producers, next for Washington-grown, then Pacific Northwest–grown, then US-grown. I want to ensure the continued availability of local products; I want to eat healthy, delicious food; and I want to preserve healthy Washington farmland, waterways, and open spaces. Ultimately, it doesn't matter if you live in Washington or Oregon, Michigan or Florida, Tuscany or Cape Town—any effort you put into finding out where your food comes from and how it's raised can only benefit you in the long run. Just ask your local farmer.

ROW CROPS

When calculating the cost of transporting our food from farm to table, we tend to leave out one intangible and yet invaluable variable: *flavor.*

Almost everything that grows tastes better and is more nutritious at the moment it is picked. There is no one who will argue that a tomato ripened in storage or even on your kitchen counter tastes better than one ripened on the vine. But in order to stand the rigors of being packed air tight, stacked high, and left in storage, produce that travels far must be bred for hardiness—not necessarily for flavor. Farmers who sell directly to consumers (whether through Community Supported Agriculture [CSA], at a farm stand, or at a farmers market) will tell you that it only makes sense to grow the most delicious varieties, or else the buyer won't come back. Buying directly from a farmer gives you the opportunity to ask questions, and it lets them know what's important to you. Armed with information, you are well prepared to vote with your dollars and support the farmers who grow what you want to eat, the way you want it raised.

According to the US Department of Agriculture's 2007 census, the number of farms in Washington grew more than 9 percent between 2002 and 2007, and the number of small farms (9 acres or less) grew a remarkable 23 percent. If we want these Washington farms to survive and prosper, it is our responsibility to support them. In return, we preserve Washington farmland and employ more than 80,000 Washingtonians. No less important, we get to enjoy an astounding variety of fresh, nutritious, and very flavorful produce.

ALVAREZ FARMS

The Chili Pepper King

Growing up in El Ranchito in Michoacán, Mexico, Hilario Alvarez's family was so poor that the only way his parents could guarantee they'd have food for their eight children was to grow it themselves. They grew primarily beans and corn, both of which could be stored for winter, and at harvest each year they'd decide whether there was enough for the family. If it looked like there was extra, they'd sell it.

Hilario left home in 1974, at nineteen, looking for a better life. He came north to Bakersfield, California, where he found farm work. He spent a year there, but jobs were hard to come by. Then a friend from home told him there was plenty of work thinning apples in Yakima, so Hilario headed north again. When he arrived, there were Help Wanted signs in front of every farm; within five years, so many migrant workers had come to stay that all the signs came down. In 1976 Hilario went home to Mexico to visit, and his sister introduced him to Maria Soledad. They married and he brought her back with him to Yakima. They now have nine children. Cristina (number six) teases, "Dad always said 'cheaper by the dozen,' but he had no idea that just applied to corn."

Today Ruben, Eduardo (Eddie), Elena, Cristina, Marisol, Hilario Jr., and Esteban Fabian work with their parents on the farm; Alicia and Oralia live in Phoenix, Arizona, where they went to college. Hilario loves that so many of his children want to farm. It's important to him that they all get a good education, but he's more than happy to have them come home afterward, telling Eddie that if

he pays attention to how to do things "and he wants to continue the business, he can keep it. I like his help here!"

Hilario does much of the "tractoring" and organizing of the farm workers. His children take and pack orders, make sure the trucks are loaded for markets, make deliveries, work the markets, and run the office. "They tell me," Hilario grins, "Dad, you take care of the farm, and we'll take care of the sales!" In addition to the Alvarezes, Hilario employs fifteen part-time workers.

The land Hilario farms in Mabton had been abandoned for fifteen years before he bought it in 1988. Right from the start, he farmed organically, but it wasn't until 1992 that he had his farm certified. Most of the farms he'd worked on in California and Washington had sprayed chemicals, but he saw a TV program many years ago about problems caused by chemical sprays among California farm workers, including birth defects and cancer. Once in charge of his own farm, there was never any question. "I wanted to keep my customers healthy, and all my workers, too."

Unaware that there was a certification process for organics, Hilario bought a radio ad that said his produce was organic. Soon after it aired he got a call from someone in Wapato who told him that if he wasn't certified organic, he had to call his produce "natural-grown." But the man offered to help Hilario earn certification, and also helped him find buyers for Hilario's (now certified organic) produce. Hilario had, to that point, just barely earned enough to make ends meet. He speaks softly and slowly, carefully pronouncing his words: "I worked for over five years for nothing, just to support my family. I buy this property, and my house, and after the payments there was nothing. But it made me happy, because if I can pay expenses, that's good."

Hilario's first piece of land was a twenty-acre parcel he bought with money borrowed from a friend. His children were young, and he did all the work himself. "And then I went organic, and it changed. I could make more money. It was the certification."

Slowly Hilario began to earn enough to send his children to college, and to buy more land. Today he farms three parcels totaling seventy acres, all within a one-mile radius. Every winter, the Alvarez family looks at what they grew the year before and what they sold. They assess the demands from the farmers markets, wholesalers, and Community Supported Agriculture (CSA) programs, and they plan their spring planting. With three or four months' notice they can plant to order—and that's what they do for the bigger wholesalers.

But it's not just the wholesalers who can request produce. One of the reasons Hilario grows such an enormous variety is that he'll try to grow anything for his customers. Years ago someone told him about squash blossoms he'd eaten on a trip. Hilario picked some for him from his farm and brought an extra case to the market. Now he sells thirty boxes a week. Customer requests inspire him to grow produce not usually associated with Washington, including peanuts, okra, and Armenian cucumbers. He grows very large tomatillos because customers told him they didn't like to peel the little ones.

Hilario leads the way across his farm, naming varieties row by row, and you can hear the

smile in his voice as he chants, "Brandywine tomatoes, cherry grape tomatoes, Green Zebra tomatoes, tomatillos, okra, peanuts, cucumbers." His youngest son, Esteban Fabian, follows close behind. He translates for his father whenever Hilario pauses to find words. Hilario reaches down to uncover a curved, deeply ridged, pale green Armenian cucumber. He picks one for each of us, and we eat them right there, crunching loudly in the one-hundred-degree sun.

The farm is very quiet except for the sound of water running along the rows of peppers. The plants are quite fragile and sunburn easily, and it's important to keep them cool and hydrated. In the heat of the day, much of the farm is dusty, but the pepper rows are moist. Gently Hilario moves the leaves aside to reveal the peppers ripening in the shade. They are clustered by color—vibrant reds, oranges, and yellows, cool whites, bright greens, and shades of purple from lavender to black—but practically every plant grows a different shape. Hilario picks a selection and drops them into my purse.

The peppers are by far his most successful crop. The Alvarez family farm stand is immediately recognizable by the hanging "rings and strings" of peppers. Hilario is rightfully proud. "I feel so happy when I see my peppers grow. Nobody else has the variety I have. Other people have tried, but it's hard. The peppers take more care than any other thing I grow." Eddie explains, "Some of the varieties we have, we hybridize ourselves. They were made right here at the farm. So other people just farm the more popular kinds; that only covers ten varieties at the most. We plant over eighty-five varieties! We hybridize for flavor, color, shape, and sweetness."

There are so many pepper varieties at Alvarez Farms that twenty-five or thirty don't even have a name. The rest, Eddie laughs, are baptized right here on the farm. Among them are Black Pasilla, Star, Snow White, Sugar Baby, Mushroom, Ghost (perhaps the hottest pepper around), and a whole assortment of different-shaped Blueberries—dark blue hot peppers with thin skins and crunchy flesh. Hilario likes to eat them raw. The first Alvarez Blueberry pepper was a small round one (hence the name). As it's cross-pollinated in Hilario's fields, he's grown them longer and longer, too.

Hilario credits the growth of his business to his peppers as well as the organic certification. It used to be that customers would buy one or two sweet peppers at a time, and it was difficult to sell the hot ones. Then he started making pepper rings using many different shapes and colors, and "people said, 'That's wonderful' and 'I've never seen anything like that.' They catch your eye when you go by, so many varieties and so many bright colors." He says some customers buy them for decoration, but most buy them to eat; he started by making twenty every week, but now sells more than one hundred per week.

Even with twenty years of experience, Hilario is still learning. A late frost at the end of May 2010 killed almost all the baby plants he'd just transplanted from the greenhouses, so he had to replant everything. The year before, the price for potatoes was so low it wasn't worth taking them to market, yet he's found he can always sell as many onions and garlic as he can grow. "Some things I lose, some I make money. Some I sell lots so I plant more, some I don't sell so I grow less the next year. It's very critical to do that. Losing and learning. You have to lose something to learn." But he refuses to waste food, so anything left over from the markets gets donated. Hilario says it makes him happy to know that hungry people are made happy.

In the shade of the packing shed it's about fifteen degrees cooler than it was in the field. Hilario sighs as he sits down. "You can only do what you can do," he says. "Sometimes I feel so tired. But with all the kids helping, it makes me happy. I want to see my fields green with vegetables! If they can't take care of the farm, I'll sell it, but if they can do it, then okay!"

Esteban Fabian stands beside his father's chair. "The farm can be difficult," he admits. "It's hard work, you have to get up early. But I love it! I can't wait for summer, for school to be out, so I can help out my dad, and go to the farmers market, see all the stuff growing. It's what I love to do. It's a good feeling, and it feels good to be part of it." Hilario looks up with a smile. He doesn't say anything—he doesn't have to.

YAKIMA PEPPERS PEPERONATA
WITH CHANTERELLES

Chef Tom Douglas, owner of numerous Seattle restaurants—including Dahlia Lounge, Lola, and Palace Kitchen—shares this recipe for his twist on peperonata, the classic Italian mix of onions, peppers, and tomatoes. It's mildly sweet and sour, and you can make it spicy-hot if you like by using hotter varieties of fresh peppers. It can be made a few days ahead; just let it come to room temperature before serving, then taste it again and adjust the salt, pepper, and vinegar. This peperonata—which has a velvety texture that's almost addictive—may be served as a stand-alone item on an antipasto dish or as a bright-flavored accompaniment to various meat or seafood dishes. The Tom Douglas Restaurants get an abundance of peppers from Tom and his wife Jackie's farm in Prosser, and also from Alvarez Farms. They buy chanterelles from Seattle's Foraged and Found Edibles.

½ cup extra-virgin olive oil, plus more for finishing

2 pounds assorted mild to medium-hot peppers (about 7 medium), seeded and cut into ½-inch pieces

8 ounces chanterelle mushrooms (or hedge-hog, crimini, or button), cleaned and roughly chopped

½ medium yellow onion, roughly chopped

1 tablespoon minced garlic

¼ cup pitted and chopped black olives, such as kalamata

¼ cup pitted and chopped green olives, such as Picholine

¼ cup finely chopped Italian parsley

3 tablespoons capers, drained and chopped

2 tablespoons red wine vinegar, plus more for seasoning

1½ teaspoons anchovy paste

Kosher salt and freshly ground black pepper

Crackers or sliced, toasted baguette, for serving

Heat the olive oil in a large skillet over high heat. Add the peppers, mushrooms, and onion and sauté, stirring frequently, until the onions are translucent, the peppers and mushrooms are quite soft, and the liquid has evaporated, about 10 minutes. If the pan seems dry, add a little more oil, then reduce the heat to medium and continue to cook, stirring, for another 10 to 12 minutes, or until the vegetables are very soft and beginning to break down. Add the garlic and sauté for 1 more minute. Remove the pan from the heat and stir in the black and green olives, parsley, capers, vinegar, and anchovy paste. Stir in enough additional olive oil to make the peperonata moist and oily. Season to taste with salt and pepper and more vinegar as desired. Transfer the peperonata to a bowl. Serve at room temperature.

MAKES 8 TO 10 APPETIZER SERVINGS (ABOUT 4 CUPS)

SWIFT RIVER TROUT WITH GREEN BEANS AND ALMONDS

Chef Andrew Wilson of Portals Restaurant at Suncadia Resort, near the high mountain town of Cle Elum, prepares mid-summer green beans with nutty-tasting brown butter and almonds. Piled on top of tender, plump fillets of local pink-fleshed Ruby trout from the Swift River, this dish is both comforting and elegantly beautiful.

7 tablespoons unsalted butter, divided

1¼ pounds haricots verts or other slender green beans

1½ tablespoons minced shallot

¾ cup sliced almonds

2 pounds trout fillets, skin on, pin bones and scales removed

Kosher salt and freshly ground black pepper

Dill sprigs, for garnish

1 lemon, halved, one half thinly sliced

In a small saucepan over low heat, melt 4 tablespoons of the butter and bring to a simmer. The butter will bubble rather noisily for a minute or so. When the bubbling subsides, remove the pan from the heat; skim and discard the milk solids that have risen to the top. Set aside.

Prepare an ice bath by filling a large bowl with ice and cold water; set it aside. Bring a large pot of salted water to a boil. Add the green beans and blanch them for 30 seconds if using haricots verts, or for about 3 minutes if using regular green beans. Drain the beans and plunge them immediately into the ice bath. When they're cold, drain them again; spread them on a clean dishtowel or paper towel to remove excess water.

In a large skillet, melt 2 tablespoons of the remaining butter over medium heat. Add the shallot and sauté until it is soft and aromatic, about 3 minutes. Add the green beans and almonds and sauté, stirring to coat the green beans with butter and toast the almonds. When the butter is beginning to brown and smell nutty, remove the pan from the heat; keep it warm while cooking the trout.

Preheat the broiler. Pat the trout fillets dry using paper towels, then season them with salt and pepper. Carefully pour all of the clarified butter into a large ovenproof skillet (one that is large enough to hold all the fillets in one layer), taking care to leave behind any browned milk solids that have sunk to the bottom of the pot. Heat the clarified butter over high heat, add the trout fillets skin side down, and sear until the skin is crispy and the edges of the fillets are cooked, about 3 minutes. (If you don't have a skillet large enough to accommodate all the fillets, sauté them in two batches, transferring to a rimmed baking sheet to finish cooking.) Cut the remaining 1 tablespoon butter into small pieces and place a piece on top of each fillet, then put the skillet (or baking sheet) under the broiler. Broil the trout until it is cooked through, about 3 minutes.

To serve, stack a sprig of dill and a lemon slice to one side on each of four plates. Lay the tail ends of the fillets on top. Spoon the beans and almonds over the fish. Drizzle with a little of the brown butter and a squeeze of lemon and serve right away.

MAKES 4 SERVINGS

MINESTRA DI VERDURE

Sabrina Tinsley, chef and co-owner of La Spiga, offers this recipe for a hearty vegetable soup with pasta that makes the most of the wealth of fresh vegetables grown in Washington. She suggests using this recipe primarily as a guide and improvising a bit using your favorite in-season vegetables. At La Spiga, the soup is puréed until it's thick and velvety, but you may opt for a different presentation by finely dicing all the vegetables and leaving them intact. It will be absolutely beautiful.

¼ cup olive oil

1 medium yellow onion, cut into large dice

1 carrot, cut into large dice

1 rib celery, cut into large dice

2 cloves garlic, peeled

2 zucchini, sliced

1 potato, peeled and diced

¼ cup peas, fresh or frozen

½ cup cooked cannellini beans

1 bunch spinach (about 8 ounces), washed and stemmed, leaves left whole

½ bunch green chard (about 4 ounces), roughly chopped

4 cups vegetable or chicken stock

3 tomatoes, diced

2 sprigs rosemary, tied with kitchen string

Salt and freshly ground black pepper

½ cup dry, small pasta such as stars, ditalini, or orzo

¼ cup extra-virgin olive oil

¼ cup grated Parmigiano-Reggiano

Heat the olive oil in a heavy-bottomed soup pot over medium heat. Sauté the onions, carrot, and celery until aromatic and beginning to soften, about 5 minutes, then add the garlic. Add the zucchini, then the potatoes, peas, and cannellini beans, then the spinach and chard, sautéing for about 3 minutes after each addition.

Add the vegetable stock, tomatoes, rosemary, and salt and pepper to taste, and bring to a boil. Reduce the heat and simmer until all the vegetables are completely tender, 25 to 35 minutes. Remove and discard the rosemary sprigs. Using an emulsion blender, purée the soup until it is very smooth. Alternatively, purée it in small batches in a food processor or blender (use caution, as hot liquids and steam rise quickly in the processor and blender). Return the soup to the pot and bring it back to a boil; add the pasta, reduce the heat slightly, and cook until tender. Ladle the soup into bowls and drizzle with the extra-virgin olive oil and Parmigiano-Reggiano.

MAKES 6 SERVINGS

BILLY'S GARDENS

A Farmer Born and Bred

"I loved farming from day one," says Billy Allstot, his cheeks creasing into a deep smile. He's standing just outside one of his greenhouses. "That's always what I wanted to do. I couldn't get out of school quick enough."

He steps out of the wind into the warmth. Inside, although it's still early in the season, tomato plants with stems as thick as a child's wrist climb at least eight feet. They hang from lines strung across the greenhouse, which is sturdily constructed from local lodgepole pine. There are fist-sized green tomatoes near the ground, and the rest of the plants are covered with bright yellow flowers. It's perfectly quiet except for a constant, quick tap-tapping: in the far corner are a pair of men walking along the rows of plants tapping the lines at the top. They do this every single day to every single plant to make sure all the flowers get pollinated. In this greenhouse alone there are 7,200 plants. Every one of them also gets pruned once a week, the leaves near the bottom removed to let in the sunlight and air. As the plants climb the strings and the fruit at the bottom ripens, the strings are lowered and moved back along the lines, and the plants climb again.

Even though he already grows more than forty varieties of heirloom, nonheirloom, and cherry tomatoes, every year Billy tries new ones. He grows only what he likes, and he's always looking for the varieties with the best flavor. He starts his plants in tiny cups in a small room so that they don't require much heat. "We baby them. We just give them everything they want," he explains. He brings in loads of compost, alfalfa hay, and peat moss, so the resulting dirt is black and rich. Water lines run underground all along the rows, and when it's cold outside, there's hot water running through them. He grafts the young plants to special disease-resistant rootstock, and then plants them in the greenhouse, where they flourish in the warm soil. The wind in the valley always blows north to south, and so Billy built doors only on the north and south walls, allowing him to control the temperature inside without fans by opening and closing some or all of the doors.

When he was growing up on his parents' farm here in Tonasket (forty acres now owned by his son, Noah), every farmer in the area either grew apples (two varieties) or raised cattle. Billy was only twenty when he took out a loan from Farmers Home Administration and planted an orchard like everyone else. A couple of years later, he had the idea to plant tomatoes between the rows of trees. Just twenty-five miles north, in British Columbia, farmers already grew vegetables and grapes along the same river, in the same soil, but no one was doing it in Okanogan County. "You wouldn't believe the upheaval that caused with my financing," he laughs.

Also early on, Billy decided to grow organic. "It just made sense to me. You know, we were fighting nature instead of working with it." Again his banker was appalled, but Billy knew it was the right thing to do.

Billy has always farmed with his eyes wide open, and he acknowledges that it's a rough way to make a living. He successfully defended his loan and rapidly expanded his farm, but eventually overextended himself borrowing money. "I went broke in the '80s. The whole thing crumbled, so I had to start all over again when I met Steph."

When Billy and his wife, Stephanie, first met, they were both recently separated and both had kids, and together they finally got on their feet again. "We're both on the same page, and that's really important. We're living for our farm." Billy points to a shiny new tractor, happily reporting that it cost twice as much as their house did.

Together they farm fifty acres they own and forty they rent from Noah. Billy has his tomatoes, as well as a huge and diverse list of other fruits and vegetables, including peaches, cherries, blueberries, strawberries, sweet and hot peppers, eggplants, sweet corn, and rhubarb. Stephanie grows a wide variety of herbs and flowers, and keeps bees, which pollinate their farm and produce honey they sell to restaurants and at some of the fifteen markets they participate in.

Billy points across the Okanogan River running through his property, up toward the bumpy, rocky, undulating mountains that contain the valley. "That's some of the oldest rock above ground on the earth right there," he says proudly. "If you get up just a ways, then you can see all the Cascades behind it. It's just gorgeous country." Noah's land reaches up that hillside, and there he's planted the first blueberry field in Okanogan County. Noah lives in Seattle and works as an engineer. For four years he's invested in irrigation, plants, and bird protection, but now that his plants are finally producing well, he's having issues with various markets that don't want to let him sell

because there's already a lot of blueberry competition. "He's had to learn everything the hard way," Billy says, "just like we did."

In order to grow his big, beautiful peaches, Billy thins them when the fruit first comes in. The ground below the trees is literally covered with tiny peaches and sticks from the winter pruning. The vegetation growing between the rows will be turned under. "It gets sort of like a big stomach here, just digesting all this organic matter, it's just like giving it a big salad to eat," explains Billy. He relies on ladybugs to keep the trees free of aphids, green manure crops like alfalfa to keep his fields green, and the birds fly through the greenhouses to keep them bug-free.

But farming in the Okanogan isn't easy. Winters are harsh—in October 2009 Billy lost eight hundred new apricot trees in a freak freeze. Summers are so hot that although he waits until the middle of June to plant peppers, eggplants, and melons, he's ready to bring them to market in August. And they only get about six inches of rain each year. "You're in survival mode every day," says Billy.

Yet Billy has never even considered living anywhere else. "It's a pretty interesting community. Everybody thinks they know everything about everybody and you get pissed off about it. But then if somebody has trouble, everybody comes in to help."

For ten years, Billy and Stephanie rented land to farm, always in Tonasket. When they could finally afford to buy, they saw a sign on the road in front of what's now Billy's Gardens, called up the owner in Canada, and made an offer. Formerly an apple orchard, it had been empty for years, so they were able to get it certified organic immediately.

Preserving and conserving the farmland in and around Tonasket is of paramount importance to both Billy and Stephanie, and they've come to realize that it will probably be the Mexican immigrants who save it. "They're the only ones who'll do the work anymore. They've got good family ethics. They're honest, hard-working, and it takes that kind of work ethic in order to hang on to it. It's a great culture." Billy is building three attached houses on his farm that will each house five workers, all air-conditioned, each with its own washer and dryer. He shakes his head at what the workers rent now. "A lot of it is very substandard housing. This'll be better than anything they've ever had. It'll be better than anything I'll ever live in!"

Billy settles into an old recliner next to a window that looks out at the river running by. "I don't do anything I don't like," he says. "That's my lifestyle. I have a low enough standard of living, there's not a lot of requirements for me. I can tell somebody to go to hell if I want to," he says with a grin. "I just do what I want to do. I don't grow any crops I don't like. I don't do it because of the money. I do it because it's something I like, and I try to figure out how to make a living out of it." And he has no plans to retire. "If you took farming away from me, that would be the ultimate torture."

Upon reflection he adds, "Winter is kind of torture for me." November is quiet on the farm. It takes Billy a couple of weeks to slow down. "But I can do it. I can hang around here, make bread and cook a good meal, watch movies, read a book." In the following months, he and Stephanie travel, too, although there are seeds to sow and baby plants to transplant and then graft and transplant again. They come and go until March. "I've been thinking maybe I'd like to have an orange grove in California or Arizona. I love to watch things grow. It's just extreme satisfaction for me. And it's exciting every day."

SPANISH HEIRLOOM TOMATO SALAD WITH HEIRLOOM TOMATO FOAM

At Matt's in the Market, Chef Chester Gerl highlights the flavor of summer-ripe tomatoes by dressing them with an airy, fresh tomato espuma, or foam. The espuma adds pizzazz, creamy texture, and a double shot of tomato flavor—but even if you don't have a whipped cream dispenser, the salad is still lovely without it. Idiazabal is a smoky, aged sheep's milk cheese from Spain. If you can't find it, substitute Manchego.

Espuma

1 to 2 ripe heirloom tomatoes (about 10 ounces total)

⅛ teaspoon powdered gelatin

½ tablespoon freshly squeezed lemon juice

¼ teaspoon salt

Salad

1½ pounds heirloom tomatoes, cored and cut into wedges

3 tablespoons extra-virgin olive oil, divided

1 tablespoon sherry vinegar

1 teaspoon minced chives

¾ teaspoon salt

½ ounce Idiazabal cheese

Italian parsley leaves, for garnish

Freshly ground black pepper

First, make the liquid that forms the base for the espuma.* Chop the tomatoes and put the pieces in a strainer set over a glass measuring cup. Use the back of a spoon to push the juice from the pulp through the strainer, until you have ½ cup juice. Put the tomato juice in a very small saucepan, sprinkle the gelatin over it and leave it to soften for 5 minutes. Then gently heat the juice, stirring, just until warm enough to melt the gelatin (the juice will thin out when this happens). Do not let the mixture come to a simmer or boil. Add the lemon juice and salt, pour the mixture into a small bowl, and let it cool to room temperature.

To assemble the salad, gently toss the tomato wedges with 2 tablespoons of the olive oil, the vinegar, chives, and salt. Divide the tomatoes between four plates. Use a vegetable peeler to cut long strips of the cheese over the top. Pour the cooled tomato juice mixture into a whipped cream canister, attach the top, and screw in a cartridge until you hear the gas release. Give the canister a few really good shakes, then hold it upside down with the tip very close to the salads, and press the lever to spray the foam on top of the tomatoes. It will come out very pale in color and very creamy and light in texture.

Garnish each salad with the parsley leaves and black pepper and drizzle with the remaining tablespoon of olive oil. Serve right away, while the foam is at its lightest.

* To make the espuma, you will need a whipped cream dispenser that uses nitrous oxide "chargers." This handy kitchen tool transforms liquids into a light, foamy mass. Most kitchen supply stores will carry several models.

MAKES 4 SERVINGS

WASHINGTON CHERRY GAZPACHO

Billy grows a lot more on his farm than just tomatoes—including more than a dozen varieties of peppers and a long list of fruits, including cherries. Here, Canlis Restaurant's Chef Jason Franey offers this recipe for a smooth and spicy twist on traditional gazpacho. Replacing the tomatoes with both fresh and dried cherries gives the soup a remarkable depth of flavor and a texture that's smooth as silk. Marinating the ingredients overnight brings out all the punch and bite of the fresh garlic, and it divides the prep time nicely into two relatively quick and easy sessions.

2 cups 1-inch cubes hearty Italian-style bread

¼ cup olive oil

2 red bell peppers, seeded and diced

1 green bell pepper, seeded and diced

2 cucumbers, peeled, seeded and diced

3 cups fresh red cherries (about 1 pound), stemmed and pitted

1⅓ cups dried sour cherries

¼ cup extra-virgin olive oil, plus additional for drizzling

2 cloves garlic, minced

3 tablespoons red wine vinegar

Salt and freshly ground black pepper

4 small slices Prosciutto (optional)

To make the croutons, toss the cubed bread with the olive oil. Toast the bread in a frying pan over medium heat, stirring often, until crisp and golden, 2 to 3 minutes.

Reserve 4 croutons for garnishing the soup (store them in an airtight container to preserve their crispness), then put the remaining croutons in a large bowl with the peppers, cucumber, fresh and dried cherries, extra-virgin olive oil, garlic, and vinegar. Stir well, cover, and marinate overnight in the refrigerator.

The following day, purée the vegetable mixture in batches in a blender or food processor until smooth. Strain through a sieve and season with salt to taste. Chill in the refrigerator until ready to serve.

To serve, ladle the soup into bowls and garnish with freshly ground black pepper, a drizzle of olive oil, a crouton, and a strip of prosciutto.

MAKES 4 SERVINGS

HEIRLOOM TOMATO PRESERVES

Chef Lisa Dupar of Lisa Dupar Catering and Pomegranate Bistro cooks vibrant summer tomatoes with vinegar and brown sugar to turn them into a flavor-packed glossy pulp; she serves them alongside her mushroom tarts (see recipe on page 148). The preserves can be made well in advance and kept in the refrigerator, although Chef Dupar suggests that they be warmed slightly before serving so that the layers of flavor will be at their brightest.

¼ teaspoon dried fennel seeds

1 tablespoon extra-virgin olive oil

2 cups diced mixed heirloom tomatoes, cored and seeded but not peeled

½ cup minced Walla Walla sweet onion

1 clove garlic, minced

¼ teaspoon salt

Pinch of cayenne pepper

¼ cup white balsamic vinegar

¼ cup light brown sugar

Toast the fennel seeds in a dry skillet for about 1 minute, tossing them occasionally to avoid over-browning, until aromatic. Grind them to a fine powder using an electric spice grinder or a mortar and pestle; set aside.

Heat the olive oil in a large, heavy-bottomed saucepan over medium-high heat. Add the tomatoes, onion, garlic, salt, cayenne, and fennel powder; bring to a rapid boil. Add the vinegar and brown sugar and return to a boil. Reduce the heat to medium low and continue cooking, stirring occasionally, until the mixture reaches the consistency of loose jam, about 30 minutes. Check the seasoning, then refrigerate the preserves if you're not going to use them right away.

MAKES ABOUT I CUP

OLSEN FARMS

The Potato Guy

It's seven o'clock on a Saturday morning in October. It's still dark, and Brent Olsen is bundled up—his long hair braided and tucked into a fuzzy wool hat, his brown canvas overalls covered with a heavy black and white wool sweater. He moves quickly, back and forth from his truck to the tables in his stand at the farmers market, panting icy puffs of air. He lifts and hauls boxes filled with a rainbow of potatoes that rumble around as he pours them into plastic crates and arranges them on long folding tables. Huge blue and white coolers filled with cuts of beef and lamb come next, and he checks their contents so that he can pull orders quickly when the market gets busy. Almost two hours later, when the opening bell rings, Brent's hands are red from the cold and the heavy lifting, his truck is empty and parked around the corner, and he is smiling and ready for his first customer.

Immediately, the market is crowded. Brent stands surrounded by a dazzling array of spotless potatoes, laughing infectiously. He remembers his regular customers' purchases, and jokes with them when they venture into new crates. He makes an effort to talk to everyone who approaches, and is constantly asked advice on how to cook the different varieties, to recommend something new, why his potatoes taste so good, and whether he'll be back next week. Everyone is glad to see him and no one turns down the opportunity for a brief chat. "It's a good feeling," he says of his hours at the market, "they like my potatoes, and they come back again and again." With his

full mountain-man beard and mustache, and his sparkling light-green eyes, Olsen looks like he used to be a musician in a grunge band. But this friendly, charming guy is passionate about potatoes, and proud to be an old-school farmer.

A fifth-generation Northwesterner, Brent always knew he wanted to farm. His grandfather, who lived on Olsen's farm until he passed away at the age of 101, grew tree fruits and grains in the Columbia Basin. Brent's family roots are in Scandinavia, where potatoes have long been a staple, and this generation seems to be infatuated with them—his sister, Nora, is a potato specialist with a PhD at the University of Idaho. Growing up, Brent watched the apple industry diversify, and he figured it was time for a similar potato revolution.

Brent's mother insisted he earn a university degree, so after receiving his bachelor's in history from Eastern Washington University, he set out to do what he really wanted: buy three hundred acres and lease another seventeen hundred in Aladdin, Washington, a ghost town in the northeast corner of the state, about thirty miles from the Idaho border. The farm sits in an isolated valley populated by wild turkeys, surrounded by mountains covered with spruce, tamarack larch, Douglas fir, and white pine. Three creeks filled with trout run through the farm, and he gets enough moisture from rain and a deep snowpack to nourish the soil. "It's a pretty special place."

There's very little rainfall in the summer, though, so Brent experimented to see what potato varieties he could farm sustainably. Some would thrive, others wouldn't, and some seed potatoes were easier to procure than others. It's difficult, he explains, to resist the urge to manage the different varieties of potatoes as one unit, especially since they're all in the same field. There are pros and cons to dry farming—Brent can't promise his plants will get exactly the number of inches of rain they need to flourish, so there are some varieties he just can't grow. But the successful ones not only have the excellent flavor that he attributes to dry farming, but they also store better, and the dry conditions help him avoid fungal diseases. And because his farm is so isolated, there are no neighboring farms to spread blight, so he doesn't need to spray.

Twenty years after starting his farm, Brent is still experimenting, rotating varieties in and out. He grows between eighteen and twenty-five different types on about twenty-three acres. Some are old varieties, like Kerr's Pink, a Scottish variety cultivated in 1907, and Bintje, a Dutch potato first cultivated in 1911. More recent varieties developed by crossbreeding at university programs include the Viking Purple by North Dakota State University in 1953 and the Yukon Gold by the University of Guelph in 1966. Some of Brent's personal favorites are German Butterballs, which have a bright yellow interior; All-Red, which are red both inside and out; and Desiree, which have a pink skin and a creamy, golden interior. Brent says he'll try to grow almost any variety. Some require longer growing seasons than he can manage, but if there's a market for them as smaller potatoes, and if they're interesting and have "high eating qualities," he'll give them a try. He says that makes every year different and exciting.

As much as Brent enjoys farming, he also loves the market and how personal it is. He loves how "fired up" people get about his potatoes, and to watch customers' reactions when they see all he has to offer, and he appreciates their willingness to try new varieties. "People can eat potatoes three meals a day," he points out, "and they get all excited, they see all these different varieties, they're almost like kids in a candy store." And he is anxious for them to know how important it is to support small farms like his, and how it benefits the local economy. He farms in Stevens County, one of the poorest in Washington state, and tries to do as much of his shopping and hiring there, "so it's a win-win." Although his nearest neighbors are a mile away, he knows he can always count on them if he needs a hand. "When you live way out where it's so rural, in some ways you have more of a sense of neighborhood. People are fired up that I'm farming there full time. I think it's a source of pride." He is quick to add that it's also important for the people who come to the markets to put a face on agriculture. Potatoes don't just show up in a bag—people see that somebody does have to pick those up and hand-sort and hand-wash them.

That "somebody" is usually Brent's mother, Merna. "I don't know how much she really sleeps," he says of the former nurse. "Sometimes if I'm driving to Spokane and I'm going to leave at four-thirty in the morning, she'll just be getting done packing restaurant orders or the little spud nut bags, making them up until about four o'clock, and then she's ready to roll with her crew again at six or seven in the morning." Brent readily admits that he usually gets all the credit, "But she's packing them and sorting them, and she's really stuck there. This

time of year it's at least forty-five minutes to Colville with the snow and ice."

In addition to his mom, Olsen employs three part- to full-time packers, and at harvest he has about ten people in the fields. He also grows a couple of acres of mixed greens that he sells in Spokane. When he gets to the west side of the mountains, he's Potato Guy, he says, but in Spokane he's selling everything from baby lettuce and arugula to Swiss chard and broccoli. Thanks to the cool nights in his valley, even the baby greens grow all summer. Brent also raises Angus cattle and sheep, and cuts about three hundred acres of hay, of which he sells about half.

For a guy who lives in an isolated valley, Brent is extremely outgoing. His favorite part of the market is talking to customers and getting to know them. He feels like "people appreciate that you've driven across snow and ice for seven hours to stand here and sell them potatoes." By the end of the year, Olsen Farms will have participated in 120 markets. "It's not like I'm ever bored," he says.

But Brent still thinks there's a lot of opportunity. "I love farming, and growing potatoes. I think there's definitely room to expand a little bit, but for right now I think I'm going to hold where I am. Burnout is definitely an issue. I mean, how much do I want to keep going and going and going? It's definitely a challenge to try to do the selling and the farming."

When Brent isn't farming or going to the markets, he has to split and cut firewood to get through the harsh Aladdin winters. As soon as there's snow on the ground, he spends any free time cross-country skiing and dog-sledding with his team of Alaskan malamutes. Even in the fall and winter, when it gets dark as early as three in the afternoon, he likes to go out with the dog sled and his headlamp. His grandfather used to ask him how he was going to "meet a lady out there like that."

As for vacations, Brent admits he doesn't take them. "I feed cows all winter. It's definitely hard, especially because I don't really have anybody to fill in for me. I drove all the tractors myself this year. I used to say to everything, you know I'll do that, I can do that, but now I realize that time is valuable, there's only so much of it. I've got to face that reality." Brent has two young nieces, and he loves their company. He laughs that they like to play farmers market, and he jokes with his mother that maybe, hopefully, in fifteen years or so they'll go to market for him.

And where does Brent see himself in another twenty years? "I'd like to be growing potatoes and doing as much farming as I can. It would be sad to think that I wasn't the Potato Guy in Seattle anymore." The truth is, it would make a lot of people sad.

FINGERLING POTATOES WITH LAVENDER, FENNEL, AND MINT

At his restaurant, Poppy, in Seattle's Capitol Hill neighborhood, Chef Jerry Traunfeld draws from a vast array of herbs and spices—many of which he grows in raised beds right outside his bright and airy restaurant's back door—to create innovative Northwest cuisine with seasonal ingredients. This aromatic side dish is a perfect example—it surprises with its sweet nose and savory flavor.

2 pounds fingerling potatoes, scrubbed and unpeeled

6 fresh lavender sprigs, or 1 teaspoon dried lavender buds

1 tablespoon kosher salt

2 teaspoons dried fennel seeds

3 tablespoons unsalted butter, at room temperature

2 teaspoons minced fresh ginger

1 teaspoon lightly chopped lavender buds, fresh or dried

Kosher salt and freshly ground black pepper

¼ cup coarsely chopped fresh mint

Cut the potatoes lengthwise into halves or quarters, depending on their size. Put them in a large pot and cover with cold water. Add the lavender sprigs and salt. Bring to a boil over high heat, then reduce the heat to medium and simmer until the potatoes are just tender when poked with the tip of a knife, about 10 minutes. Drain the potatoes and discard the lavender.

Heat a large skillet over medium heat. Add the fennel seeds and toast them, tossing occasionally to avoid over-browning, until they are aromatic and a shade darker in color, about 1 minute. Add the butter, ginger, and lavender buds. Add the potatoes and cook, tossing often, until they are hot and the flavors have a chance to meld, about 5 minutes. Season to taste with salt and pepper. Add the mint, toss to combine, and serve.

MAKES 6 SERVINGS

POMMES ALIGOT

This side dish from Executive Chef Daisley Gordon at Marché Bistro and Wine Bar is a cross between the most decadent mashed potatoes and the richest cheese fondue you've ever dreamed about. Chef Gordon recommends having all your ingredients ready before you start cooking. To save a little time, you can peel and cut the potatoes and store them in water in the refrigerator up to two days ahead; you can also grate the cheese and store it cold and airtight. The dish will be at its most luscious when served fresh and piping hot.

1½ pounds Yukon Gold potatoes (about 5 medium), peeled and cut into 1-inch dice

3 cloves garlic, thinly sliced

4 tablespoons unsalted butter

6 tablespoons heavy cream, divided

12 ounces young Cantal cheese or sharp cheddar cheese, grated (about 4 cups)

Sea salt

Put the potatoes and garlic into a 2-quart saucepan, cover with cold water, and bring to a boil over medium-high heat. Reduce the heat to medium-low and simmer gently until the potatoes are tender, about 5 minutes, then drain the potatoes, being careful not to lose the garlic pieces. Pass the potatoes and garlic through a food mill or potato ricer and into a bowl.

Put the butter and 3 tablespoons of the heavy cream back into the empty saucepan over medium heat; heat until the butter melts and the whole mixture foams. Add the puréed potatoes and stir the mixture with a wooden spoon to blend. Cover with a lid or plate and set aside in a warm place.

Heat a large nonstick pan over medium-high heat. Add the remaining 3 tablespoons of heavy cream and bring to a simmer. Add the grated cheese and stir until melted, then add the reserved potatoes and mix thoroughly with the wooden spoon. The cheese and potatoes will combine into a smooth mixture with a slightly stringy quality from the melted cheese. Season with additional salt as needed and serve right away.

MAKES 4 TO 6 SERVINGS AS A SIDE DISH

TRUFFLE POTATO SALAD

Tulio Ristorante in downtown Seattle is known for being comfortable yet elegant, so this beautiful, aromatic dish is a perfect contribution from Chef Walter Pisano. The pungent earthiness of the black truffles and the fresh bite of the parsley, chives, and shallots show-case beautifully against the buttery Yukon Golds. Fresh local black truffles are available from foragers in winter, or you can use preserved truffles (which come in jars as small as 1 ounce), although their flavor is much more mild. Truffle oil is simply olive oil infused with truffles, and it packs a surprising punch of flavor that can be used any time of year.

4 medium Yukon Gold potatoes (about 1¼ pounds)

2 tablespoons black truffle oil

2 tablespoons extra-virgin olive oil

1½ tablespoons minced shallots

1 tablespoon minced fresh black truffles or jarred black truffles in oil

1 teaspoon white balsamic vinegar

1 teaspoon freshly squeezed lemon juice

2 tablespoons finely chopped Italian parsley

2 tablespoons finely chopped chives

Sea salt and ground white pepper

Peel the potatoes, square off the edges, and cut them into a uniform small dice, just slightly larger than ¼-inch square. Keep the diced potatoes submerged in a bowl of cold water to prevent them from turning brown. Bring a pot of salted water to a boil over high heat. Drain the diced potatoes, add them to the boiling water, and bring the water back up to a boil. Reduce the heat to medium-low and simmer gently until the potatoes are tender but not mushy, about 5 minutes. Drain the potatoes well and spread them on a baking sheet to cool. If you're not ready to proceed with the dressing, refrigerate the potatoes until you're ready to dress them.

To make the dressing, combine the truffle oil, olive oil, shallots, truffles, vinegar, and lemon juice in a bowl and whisk together well.

About 1 hour before serving, carefully fold the dressing into the potatoes and leave to marinate, covered, in the refrigerator or at room temperature. Just before serving, fold in the parsley and chives and add salt and pepper to taste.

MAKES 4 SERVINGS

PELINDABA LAVENDER

The Accidental Farmer

The first time someone suggested to Stephen Robins that he visit San Juan Island, he said he had no interest in the Caribbean. But after just one week there he set about moving his company to Seattle and planning his retirement on the island.

It's no surprise Stephen hadn't heard of the San Juans: he was born and raised in South Africa. He began medical school there in 1960 and became involved in the anti-apartheid student movement. When the government encouraged him to move elsewhere, he left for England, where he had to begin his training again. He joined the Royal Navy to pay for medical school and a postgraduate degree, and after qualifying, spent five years in the Far East, serving mostly in Hong Kong and Singapore. Upon his return to England in 1975, he found it at the height of a depression, and set off again, this time for Canada.

Stephen spent a year in Toronto as a medical adviser to a large pharmaceutical company, then ran international clinical studies for a Palo Alto, California, company. He discovered that his real interest was in medical communications, and after another job change took him to Southern California, he started a company to do just that. He spent the next ten years developing written materials and video and creating task forces. He would only take on work that fulfilled certain criteria: no "me too" products or technology, there had to be a worthwhile reason for it to exist, and "it had to be safer, or more effective or more convenient for the condition, or more comfortable for the patient, or less expensive for everybody."

Stephen was in a meeting with a company from Bothell when he first heard about the San Juans. The next time he met with them was in Seattle, and afterward Stephen took the ferry to Friday Harbor. He was so taken with the island, he set in motion a four-year plan that involved opening a branch of his company in Seattle, buying a ten-acre property inland on San Juan, slowly moving himself into a consultant position, and finally giving the business to his employees. His plan was then to write, sail the islands, and enjoy the peace and quiet.

By the end of 1997 he was winding down his involvement in his company. He had bought another piece of property on the west side of the island and started building a house there. A few years earlier he'd added ten acres adjacent to the original property to protect the view, and now he had to decide what to do with it all when he moved. He considered selling it, but realized how much he loved the serenity of the little valley. Never one to take the easy route, Stephen decided to make it an open space preservation project. The challenge, of course, was to make it self-sustaining. "It wasn't just sustainable agriculture, which was what I was interested in at the time," he says, "but make it self-sustaining in an economic sense as well. If I had just left the land open, it would have needed support, if for nothing but paying property taxes."

The problem with a lot of protected land, Stephen knew, was that it was impossible for most people to access. He loved that so much of the heritage of the island is farming and big open spaces, and he wanted to honor that.

To give people a reason to visit, and to make the land self-sustainable, he decided to farm it. He named it Pelindaba, which means "place of great gatherings" in Zulu. He hoped for "great gatherings of crops and great gatherings of people." He tackled this project, even though he was retired, the same way he'd done everything before.

"I set four criteria," Stephen explains. "First of all, I wanted to grow something that no one else on the island was growing, because I wasn't doing it for a living and others were and I didn't want to compete with them. I wanted to complement them." Second, because San Juan Island is in a rain shadow, he wanted to put in a crop that did not require much water. Third was no fertilizer, because everyone in the local community relies on drinking wells and everything put on the land ends up in the water supply. And the fourth criterion was that the crop had to be economically viable on only twenty acres. "Put everything through that sieve," he explains, "and the only thing that came out the other end was lavender." He adds, "It's perfect. You don't have to tend it much. It takes care of itself. You don't have to water it. The plants are perennials. You need no fertilizing. You just need to harvest once a year, and you can do it in stages."

Although he had no experience farming, Stephen rolled up his sleeves and talked to the local extension agent (a farming expert employed by Washington State University who helps people in rural areas). He did an enormous amount of time-consuming research (this was pre-Google), and every time he found another book on the subject it contradicted many of the things he'd read before. Stephen remembers meeting David Christie, who was at the time farming lavender on the English

Channel island of Jersey. Christie told him he was going to have to learn for himself, and "never a truer word was spoken."

Stephen's plan was to sell the flower stalks and buds, and because that market was limited, to distill lavender oil and hydrosol (the floral water that comes out in the distillation process) and sell those raw materials as well. His initial investment in the farm was substantial, because he had to install a field-wide French drain system. The only thing that kills lavender is a fungal root rot, so it's imperative that the soil drains well. Then, just as he was getting ready to start distilling in 2001, an international price war over lavender oil broke out, and the price ended up below Stephen's break-even point. When he realized that he wasn't going to be able to sell the raw materials and make enough to support the land, his only choice was to make the product himself.

"So all of a sudden this venture took on a huge cost structure," Stephen says. To protect his investment, he had to invest more. "I had to create a huge marketing structure to generate the revenues to cover the costs. It was literally a choice to either stay small and fold, or get much larger than I'd ever planned to and be successful." The decision was an easy one, because it was so fascinating. "The more I read, the more interesting it became." He loved that lavender has a rich and ancient history and so many powerful properties: It's self preserving, fragrant, an excellent topical anesthetic, a sedative, an antiseptic, a very good oil solvent, an insect repellant, and, of course, a culinary herb that works well on both the savory and sweet side of the palate.

Applying the same standards he applied to his previous work in the medical and pharmaceutical fields, Stephen studied the science and

set up production, emphatically stating that he wasn't going to sell anything that he didn't believe in, make any claims he hadn't satisfied sufficiently for himself, and would frame everything in the appropriate language.

In the summer of 2001 Stephen opened a store on the farm and sold fifty different lavender products. By summer 2010 he had two hundred and fifty lavender products made with the pure certified-organic lavender he grows and distills himself. In the process of growing the farm and the business, Stephen has explored the fields of culinary arts, personal care, therapy, decorative arts, and household products. He has learned farming, manufacturing, and retailing. He opened and ran a retail shop in downtown Seattle and one in Friday Harbor with a cafe, until he decided that working eighteen-hour days in retirement wasn't reasonable. "I cannot remember," he says, "when I was as intellectually challenged as much as this to make it actually work." For several years he allowed the whole venture to grow organically, continuously evolving his strategic long-term plan for Pelindaba. In the end, not wanting to spend his time growing and expanding a string of retail stores (he had by this time opened two additional stores on the mainland), Stephen closed the off-island stores and is now slowly expanding Pelindaba's retail presence by offering retail licensing opportunities for others to operate Pelindaba stores instead. The first opened in downtown Seattle, the second in Santa Rosa, California.

The farm itself is always open, even when the gatehouse store is closed. It is truly an open space. All summer a steady stream of cars come down the quiet lane and turn into the grassy parking lot. The cutting fields include five varieties of lavender, with dozens more in the exhibition garden. The fresh flowers available for cutting and planting draw a lot of "agritourists." In the main field, Pelindaba grows primarily the Grosso and Provence varieties for oil production and sachet buds. For culinary use, buds are harvested early, before the surprisingly bitter lavender essential oil has a chance to accumulate. A devastating fire in early summer 2009 destroyed Pelindaba's production facility on the farm, which included the distillery and a commercial kitchen, but they are rebuilding. In the meantime, the new distillery is set up behind the gatehouse store and they've rented temporary space in the town of Friday Harbor, where they make their value-added products.

While Stephen admits that his retirement is not as it's generally envisioned, and not as he had envisioned it himself, he is adamant. "I have zero regrets. You do what's interesting and what you want to do. I don't feel like I've worked in my life. It's been this wonderful intellectual trip, along with a lot of nonintellectual experiences, and I always just followed what I wanted to do." He describes his current state as "re-tired." He's even back living on the farm. "This is worth doing. I'm creating something that people enjoy. It's fun to do and gives pleasure. What more could you want out of life?"

ROASTED BEET SALAD WITH PORT-LAVENDER VINAIGRETTE

This lavender-scented salad comes from Chef Jack Strong, from his time as executive chef at The Dining Room at the Salish Lodge & Spa in Snoqualmie. Roasting brings out the natural sweetness of the beets, which is intensified by a quick marinade in the port vinaigrette; creamy goat cheese offers the perfect counterbalance. The restaurant gets much of its fresh, seasonal vegetables and fruits from Full Circle farm and its raw fireweed honey from Mr. B's in Redmond.

Salad

1 bunch baby red beets (about 5)

1 bunch baby yellow beets (about 5)

Olive oil, for coating the beets

2 tablespoons chopped toasted hazelnuts

½ head frisée lettuce, leaves cut into 1-inch pieces

8 ounces goat cheese

2 red radishes, thinly sliced

16 small fresh basil leaves

Salt and freshly ground black pepper

Vinaigrette

1 cup port wine

3 sprigs fresh lavender, or 1½ teaspoons dried lavender buds

1 shallot, minced

1 tablespoon minced chives

1 tablespoon honey

1 tablespoon red wine vinegar

1 teaspoon Dijon mustard

½ cup extra-virgin olive oil

Salt and freshly ground black pepper

Preheat the oven to 325 degrees F. Cut the greens from the beets, but leave a short bit of the stems still attached—this will help keep the beets from bleeding their juices as they cook. Wash and dry them well, then coat the beets lightly with olive oil and season with salt. Wrap them loosely in aluminum foil and bake until tender, about 45 minutes.

Meanwhile, make the vinaigrette. Add the port and the lavender to a small saucepan and simmer over medium heat until the port has reduced to ¼ cup. Strain it into a medium bowl and set it aside to cool. When the liquid is at room temperature, add the shallot, chives, honey, vinegar, and mustard and then slowly whisk in the extra-virgin olive oil until the dressing is emulsified. Season to taste with salt and pepper.

Periodically check the beets; when a paring knife pierces the beets and slips back out easily, they are done. Once the beets are tender, remove them from the oven, unwrap them and set them aside until they are cool enough to handle, then remove the delicate outer skin with a small paring knife (or slip them off with gloved hands). While the beets are still warm, cut them into quarters. Put the red beets in one small bowl and the yellow beets in another, and toss each with 2 tablespoons of the vinaigrette. Season to taste with salt and pepper and refrigerate for at least 30 minutes to marinate.

To serve, sprinkle the hazelnuts onto four salad plates. Toss the frisée with about 1 tablespoon of the vinaigrette and place a mound of it in the center of each plate. Crumble the goat cheese on top of the frisée and arrange the beets, radish slices, and basil leaves around it.

MAKES 4 SERVINGS

PROVENCAL HERB–DUSTED ALBACORE WITH LENTILS AND CUMIN-ONION JAM

Chef Danielle Custer uses only local, sustainably caught albacore tuna from Fishing Vessel St. Jude *to prepare this eclectic dish at TASTE Restaurant in the Seattle Art Museum. The spicy lentils and cumin-scented onions showcase the silky tuna beautifully, and the presentation is dinner party–perfect. For the mixed greens, Chef Custer uses a combination of spinach, wild arugula, sorrel, fennel tops, parsley, mint, and thinly sliced butter lettuce or romaine.*

Cumin-Onion Jam

3 tablespoons extra-virgin olive oil

1½ cups thinly sliced yellow onion

2 cloves garlic, minced

1 teaspoon cumin seeds, toasted and ground

1 tablespoon sherry vinegar

Lentils

5 ounces slab bacon

1 cup finely diced sweet onion, such as Walla Walla

1 tablespoon grated fresh ginger

1 large clove garlic, minced

½ jalapeño pepper, minced

1 tablespoon Madras curry powder

Pinch of cinnamon

1 cup French green "du Puy" lentils, rinsed under cold water

2 cups chicken stock

1 bay leaf

Kosher salt

Tuna and Salad

1 to 1½ pounds albacore tuna loin

1 tablespoon ground dry lavender

1 tablespoon herbes de Provence

Kosher salt and freshly ground black pepper

2 tablespoons olive oil

2 cups mixed greens, washed and dried

¼ cup extra-virgin olive oil, plus more for drizzling

2 tablespoons freshly squeezed lemon juice

To make the onion jam, heat the olive oil in a medium sauté pan over medium-low heat. Add the onion and sauté until it is very tender and beginning to turn golden, about 30 minutes. The idea is to "melt" the onion by cooking it for a lengthy amount of time over low heat, so adjust the heat as necessary and stir often. Add the garlic and sauté for 5 minutes. Add the cumin and vinegar and sauté for an additional 5 minutes. Set aside to cool.

While the onion cooks, make the lentils. First cut the bacon into "lardons," narrow strips about 1 inch long and ¼ inch thick. Slowly render the bacon in a medium pot over medium-low heat until the lardons are crisp. Use a slotted spoon to remove them from the fat, and drain them on paper towels. Pour off most of the bacon fat, increase the heat to medium, then add the onion and sauté until translucent, stirring occasionally, about 7 minutes. Add the ginger, garlic, and jalapeño and sauté for 1 minute, stirring constantly. Add the curry powder and cinnamon, stir to mix well, then add the lentils and sauté them, stirring, until the mixture is very fragrant, about 1 minute. Add the chicken stock and the bay leaf, increase the heat to medium-high, and bring the mixture to a simmer. Adjust the heat so that the lentils are simmering gently; cook them until most of the liquid has been absorbed and the lentils are tender, about 30 minutes. Add the bacon, season to taste with salt, and set aside.

To prepare the tuna, cut the loin in half, if necessary, so that it will fit in a large, heavy skillet (preferably cast iron). Season the tuna on all sides with the lavender, herbes de Provence, and salt and pepper. Heat the olive oil in the skillet over medium-high heat. Sear the loins on each side just until they are golden brown. Let the loins rest on a cutting board while you assemble the greens.

In a medium bowl, toss the greens with the extra-virgin olive oil and lemon juice. Season to taste with salt and pepper. Divide the lentils between the plates and top with the dressed greens. Cut the tuna on a slight angle into ¼-inch-thick slices and arrange on the greens. Top with a forkful of the onion jam and drizzle with a bit more extra-virgin olive oil.

MAKES 4 SERVINGS

ROASTED DUCK BREAST WITH LAVENDER, CORIANDER, AND FENNEL

At Crush, chef/owner Jason Wilson serves this spice-rubbed duck with corn pudding and roasted wild mushrooms, but it would pair equally well with roasted potatoes and a simple green salad. The well-seasoned, crispy skin protects the juicy, tender meat permeated with fresh orange and brandy. The layers of flavor elevate this impressive-to-serve dish.

¾ tablespoon coriander seeds

¾ tablespoon fennel seeds

2 tablespoons lavender buds

1 tablespoon sea salt or kosher salt

3 pounds large duck breasts

¼ cup brandy

Zest of 2 oranges (about 2 tablespoons)

1 tablespoon fresh thyme leaves

Freshly ground black pepper

In a small heavy skillet over medium heat, toast the coriander and fennel seeds until they are lightly browned and aromatic, stirring or shaking constantly, about 2 minutes. Let them cool, then grind them with the lavender and salt using a spice grinder or a mortar and pestle.

Trim any excess fat from the duck breasts, then use a sharp knife to score a crisscross pattern in the skin. This will take a bit of care; you want to cut all the way through the fat but not cut into the flesh. Rub the spice mixture into the skin of the duck (rub some into the spaces created by the scoring as well) and then place the breasts, skin side down, in a dish large enough to hold them all without overlapping. Drizzle the brandy over the flesh side, then sprinkle the orange zest, thyme, and pepper on top. Cover and let marinate, refrigerated, for 30 minutes.

Preheat the oven to 350 degrees F. Heat a heavy ovenproof skillet (preferably stainless steel) over medium-low heat. Add the duck breasts to the hot pan, skin side down, and allow the fat to render very slowly until the skin is crisp and thin. Don't be tempted to shortcut this process—it should take about 10 minutes.

Turn the breasts over so that the skin side is up, then put the pan into the oven and bake for about 4 minutes (for medium doneness). Take the duck from the pan, tent lightly with foil, and allow it to rest for 5 minutes. Slice each breast and fan the slices slightly, dividing the meat equally between warmed dinner plates.

MAKES 4 TO 6 SERVINGS

SPARKLING LAVENDER LEMON DROP

Lisa Dupar, chef and owner of Lisa Dupar Catering and Pomegranate Restaurant, fondly remembers the first time Dry Soda Co. founder Sharelle Klaus came up from Tacoma with samples of her new line of sodas. Says Lisa, "I remember instantly thinking 'She's going to skyrocket to the top with this wonderful line of non-alcoholic, upscale sodas.'" This recipe makes extra lavender syrup, which will keep indefinitely—use it to make more cocktails or to sweeten tea.

1 cup sugar

1 cup water

1 tablespoon dried lavender buds

Superfine sugar, for the rims of the glasses

2 ounces (¼ cup) Lavender Dry Soda, chilled

4 ounces (½ cup) lemon vodka, preferably Absolut Citron

1½ ounces (3 tablespoons) freshly squeezed lemon juice

1 ounce (2 tablespoons) triple sec

2 splashes black raspberry liqueur, preferably Chambord

2 twists fresh orange peel

To make the lavender syrup, start at least a couple of hours before you need it so that the syrup can chill thoroughly. Put the sugar, water, and lavender into a small saucepan over medium-high heat. Stir until the sugar has dissolved completely, then bring the mixture to a full boil. Remove from the heat and let the lavender steep for 5 minutes. Strain and chill.

Rim 2 martini glasses with superfine sugar by wetting a clean kitchen towel and laying it on the counter. Have ready a plate or shallow bowl with at least ¼ inch of superfine sugar spread on it. Turn each glass over and press it to the wet towel to moisten the rim, then gently place the rim of the glass into the sugar. Turn the glass gently a couple of times to get the sugar to stick. Set the glass upright and add the lavender dry soda, being careful not to disturb the sugar rim. Repeat with the second glass.

Put 2 ounces (¼ cup) of the lavender syrup, the lemon vodka, lavender syrup, lemon juice, triple sec, and black raspberry liqueur into a shaker with ice, shake, and strain into the glasses. Add the orange twists and serve right away.

MAKES 2 SERVINGS

BLUEBIRD GRAIN FARMS

Amber Waves of Grain

Three large mule deer graze on dropped grain behind the towering storage bins. The rich brown late-September hills are covered with patches of grass, and the ground crunches beneath our feet as we walk along the hillside above Bluebird Grain Farm's granary, trying not to startle the deer. Bluebird is nestled in a little valley just outside Winthrop, and both the land above and below belong to the Forest Service. Sam and Brooke Lucy appear to be running a heavenly buffet here for migrating mule deer. On the menu: dark northern winter rye, hard dark northern red wheat, spring soft white wheat, and the farm's signature grain, emmer wheat (also known as farro).

The Lucys do everything from the plow to the table, from growing their grain on two hundred acres they lease in the Upper Methow Valley to harvesting it and bringing it to the granary to clean, mill, and package. Brooke explains, "As a really small farm, it is critical for us to add value in every single step, to control the quality, and to make it absolutely the best possible product that we can."

To that end, the granary's storage bins are wood, because it allows the grain to breathe as it dries after harvest. On most conventional farms, grain is fumigated every couple of weeks because it's stored in tin silos where it can get moldy. The Lucys see this fumigation as a serious health concern, and have made it a priority to avoid it. They believe that the organic principles of farming are fundamental to making the highest quality food, and since their organic practices continue after harvest, they can guarantee their grains stay that way.

Once the grain is dry and cured, it gets cleaned, at which point it's ready to be eaten or milled. It's a lot of work to fill and start and stop the various pieces of machinery, and to clean, fill, and package the grains, but each week they clean and mill just what they need. "We believe that people need to have the absolute best food," Brooke explains. "Food is the foundation of our health—our community's health and our individual health. And so we need to take that much care in your food as a producer. We need to take the time to make sure that you get it fresh, because when it's fresh, it's more nutritious." As soon as grain gets milled it begins to oxidize, and after three or four weeks it has lost much of its nutritional value.

Bluebird can store the whole grain and mill it to order because whole grains "have their own little storage capsules. So unless you crack them or mill them, they are totally nutritious." Still, the Lucys pride themselves on making sure they sell only the current year's crop. Around mid-January or February, in order to plan for his spring planting, Sam looks at their field capacity and at how well they're moving through the previous year's harvest. If they need to, they sell to organic bakeries to ensure their granary will be empty in time for the upcoming harvest.

The last machine in Bluebird's production line funnels the grain into little packages, which they sell to grocery stores, health and specialty stores, farmers markets, and directly to customers via UPS, which comes to the granary door every day. When Bluebird Grain Farms began, the Lucys had no idea how much they'd be able to sell online, from the farm, or at the market, so they jumped in everywhere. "Basically," Brooke says, "we just tossed every option that was possible in the air, and said okay, let's see where it lands." The biggest benefit they get from being at the farmers market is exposure, but it's been difficult, because they want to be home for their young children. They know they need to keep networking and marketing, and getting to know their customers, because there are new small grain farms starting all the time. It's important for them to be established as a very high quality producer that people will think about first when they're thinking grains. As a small producer, they know there's room for competition, but the Lucys want to be successful close to home. "My ideal vision," Brooke says, "is to make sure everything we grow stays in the Northwest."

Brooke grew up in Wenatchee, where her parents had sixty acres of cherry trees that provided a partial income, but she never imagined she'd end up farming. An avid Nordic skier, Brooke came to Winthrop after college to spend a winter skiing. Not only was Sam her neighbor, but it turned out he had also skied in college, and they had many friends and acquaintances in common. "And it was a long winter," she laughs. Before Bluebird, Brooke was an educator. Her last jobs before starting Bluebird were as the director of a small independent school that she helped start, writing grants for various nonprofit organizations, and as a backcountry ranger for the Forest Service.

Sam grew up on a six-hundred-acre farm in New Hampshire that his family has farmed since the Revolutionary War. His sister married a Washingtonian and came to live out here, and when Sam came to visit, he fell in love with the area. He got a job as an apprentice to a grain farmer and stayed. Brooke describes him as having "a very intimate relationship with nature and with farming, and that's certainly his path and his passion. And it's driven his interest particularly to food. He's a real purist when it comes to food and wanting access to the cleanest, most nutritious food." Sam's other love is writing fiction, short stories in particular. He's published a collection called *Holding Ground*, and his work has appeared in a number of magazines. Prior to starting Bluebird, he had his own business doing land restoration. He'd go into fallow farmland and either restore it to a more natural state or he'd get it back into farm production.

When Sam and Brooke decided to start a family, they were working five jobs between the two of them. It quickly became clear that it would be difficult for them to make a living in the area, but they really wanted to stay. They loved living in a small rural community and feeling connected to their neighbors, and at the same time they enjoyed the independence of living in a place as wild and beautiful as the Methow Valley. They still treasure their access to that wilderness, and ski, hike, and run from their back door, happy to be raising their children in a place so unspoiled there are still bears around their creek. So, Brooke says, "We put our heads together and thought about what our value system was and what was really important and what we loved to do. And this is what we came up with."

Although Brooke had just become certified as a school counselor, the Lucys realized that it made the most sense if they were both doing the same thing, and supporting the momentum of that business. Brooke acknowledges that it could have been difficult to work together, but she believes they've been successful because the business has been successful. "I think it has helped us, given us confidence in our roles. Sam does the farming and the processing. I do the customer service, the marketing, and the finances. If it was failing, I think it would be stressful." At the beginning, the Lucys were so focused on learning the business and wanted to stay in the area so badly they pretty much had to figure everything out, Brooke recalls.

In his land restoration business, Sam had grown various grains as a way to improve the soil, sometimes as a green crop for out-competing weeds and sometimes as green manure—the term farmers use for plant material that builds the soil in much the same way as animal manure. The grains are allowed to sprout, and are then incorporated back into the soil as quickly as possible, before they draw the precious nutrients out of the soil.

Because Sam felt comfortable growing grain, understood its life cycle, and already owned some of the equipment they'd need to farm it, the Lucys decided to become grain farmers. In 2005, they grew small plots of each type of grain they were considering. They'd received a sample of farro from a professor who was running a research program on ancient grains and was retiring. The university was not planning to continue the program, so the professor was giving away the seeds. "The farro really just spoke for itself," Brooke remembers. They grew it, harvested it, thought the seeds were incredible, and wondered what it was.

Emmer wheat, or *Triticum dicoccon*, is commonly known as farro. It was one of the first cereals domesticated in the Fertile Crescent, and the primary wheat grown in Asia, Africa, and Europe for the first 5,000 years of recorded agriculture (over 17,000 years ago).

The Lucys knew that as small farmers, their challenge was to find a niche where they could offer something unique that people could get excited about. Brooke went online, and quickly realized what an incredible culinary scene there was around farro in Northern Italy; it had a growing presence in the United States, too, particularly within the chef community. The nutritious grain is prized for its nutty flavor and chewy, toothsome texture when cooked. Hedging their bets, they chose a couple of heritage varieties of wheat and rye to grow as well.

In addition to the grains they grow to harvest on about half their acreage, Sam also plants flax, buckwheat, mustard, clover, and peas as cover crops, which are tilled back into the soil. And every year, some of their land lies fallow. Sam strongly believes that the quality of the final product begins with the soil. He invests a great deal of time and energy "learning about it, knowing about it, and understanding the properties of it." They test the soil throughout the year, constantly monitoring it so that they can put back what they take out of it. That, Brooke explains, is "the balance of organic farming."

Five years into it, Brooke knows she and Sam made the right decision for their family when they started Bluebird Grain. But, she says, "One thing that I totally underestimated when we started was how much time and energy this would take." And she has no expectations that one day her daughters will take over. "I feel like if we can support our family and provide this premium product to our friends and neighbors, then that's enough . . . it's been a success."

FARRO RISOTTO WITH MORELS

Vuong Loc, chef and owner of restaurants June and Portage in Seattle, offers this recipe for farro cooked risotto-style. The hearty grain cooks more slowly than rice does so you may want to recruit someone to help you stir, but the result is a chewy, nutty, creamy, decadent dish studded with earthy morels and the heady scent of truffles—well worth the effort. If you can't find fresh morels, substitute 2 ounces of dried morels, reconstituted, and use the mushroom broth they make to replace some of the chicken stock.

¼ cup extra-virgin olive oil

8 ounces morels, rinsed several times and sliced into rings

1 cup minced yellow onion

1¾ cups farro

2 sprigs fresh thyme

1 cup white wine

About 10 cups hot chicken stock

3 ounces grated Parmesan cheese (about 1 cup), divided

2 tablespoons cold unsalted butter, cut into pieces

Truffle oil, for drizzling (about ¼ teaspoon per plate)

Salt and freshly ground black pepper

Aged balsamic vinegar, for drizzling

Heat the olive oil almost to the smoking point in a large heavy-duty saucepan over high heat. Add the morels and sauté until they've browned, about 2 minutes, then use a slotted spoon to remove the mushrooms, leaving some oil in the pan. Season the mushrooms with salt and pepper and set them aside. Add the onion to the oil in the pot and lower the heat to medium. Sweat the onion until it is tender and translucent, stirring often, about 4 minutes. Add the farro, thyme, and a pinch of salt; stir to toast the farro for 2 minutes.

Add the wine and stir to loosen any bits from the bottom of the pan. Cook until the wine has been completely absorbed. Add the hot stock, 1 cup at a time, allowing the liquid to be absorbed before adding more. Stir vigorously every minute or so. The farro may need extra stock or hot water to reach the desired consistency. Also, you may need to season it lightly as you go, depending on how salty your stock is (remember that you will be adding cheese at the end, which will also contribute to the saltiness of the dish).

After about 55 minutes, when the farro is cooked al dente and the liquid in the pot is thick and starchy, remove the pot from the heat. Discard the thyme sprigs, then stir in the reserved mushrooms, half the cheese, and the butter; allow the risotto to rest, covered, for 5 minutes before serving. Check the seasoning, transfer to a warm serving bowl, drizzle with truffle oil, top with the remaining cheese, and drizzle with balsamic vinegar.

MAKES 2 TO 3 MAIN COURSE SERVINGS
OR 6 SERVINGS AS A SIDE DISH

ROASTED CAULIFLOWER FARRO SALAD

Anson and Jenny Klock, chefs and owners of Picnic, share this recipe for a hearty salad that combines chewy, nutty farro, tender roasted cauliflower, crunchy pistachios, and green olives with a light lemon vinaigrette. The addition of tiny bits of salty-sour preserved lemon (Anson recommends making your own using Meyer lemons, the wonderfully aromatic variety that is a cross between a mandarin orange and a lemon) adds a punch of flavor.

Vinaigrette

Rind of ¼ preserved lemon, very finely diced (about 2 teaspoons)

½ tablespoon preserved lemon syrup from the jar

2 tablespoons plus 2 teaspoons champagne vinegar

¼ teaspoon Dijon mustard

½ tablespoon minced fresh thyme leaves

½ cup extra-virgin olive oil

Salt and freshly ground black pepper

Salad

1 cup farro

1 medium head cauliflower

2 tablespoons olive oil

½ cup Castelvetrano olives, pitted and chopped

½ cup Italian parsley leaves, torn

½ cup roasted pistachio nuts

Salt and freshly ground black pepper

To make the vinaigrette, combine the lemon rind, lemon syrup, vinegar, mustard, and thyme in a small bowl. Whisk together, then gradually whisk in the extra-virgin olive oil. Season to taste with salt and pepper. (This recipe makes a generous ½ cup of vinaigrette. Leftovers can be stored in the refrigerator for up to 2 weeks.)

Preheat the oven to 400 degrees F. Bring a large pot of heavily salted water to a rolling boil. Add the farro and cook for 5 minutes, stirring often to make sure the grains are not sticking to the pan or to each other. Reduce the heat to low, cover the pot, and simmer until the farro is al dente, about 45 minutes. Drain the farro and spread it onto a baking sheet to cool.

Meanwhile, split the head of the cauliflower, remove the core, and break it into individual florets, each about the size of a quarter. Toss with the olive oil and season with salt and pepper. Spread the florets on a baking sheet and roast them in the oven until dark brown and crispy, about 40 minutes, stirring and turning the florets about every 10 minutes so that they roast evenly. Remove the cauliflower from the oven and set it aside to cool.

To assemble the salad, combine the cooked farro, cauliflower, olives, parsley, and pistachio nuts. Add vinaigrette to taste, starting with ¼ cup and adding more as desired. Season to taste with salt and pepper. Serve warm, at room temperature, or cold.

MAKES 6 SERVINGS AS A SIDE DISH

RYE PRETZELS

Seattle restaurant Poppy's former pastry chef, Dana Cree, used rye flour from Bluebird Grain Farms to make these soft and chewy bite-size pretzels. Plump, golden, and savory, they have just enough rye and caraway to set them apart from the crowd. Five dozen pretzels may sound like a lot, but they're quick and fun to make, and even quicker to disappear. Irresistible plain, they're even more addictive dipped in a top-quality Dijon mustard.

4 cups bread flour	10 cups water
½ cup rye flour	1 cup baking soda
½ teaspoon active dry yeast	1 large egg
2 teaspoons kosher salt	1 tablespoon water
1 tablespoon ground caraway seed	Coarse sea salt, for sprinkling
2 cups warm water (90 degrees F)	
3 tablespoons unsalted butter, cut into pieces, at room temperature	

Put the bread flour, rye flour, yeast, salt, and caraway into the bowl of a stand mixer. Use the dough hook attachment to stir together.

On very low speed, add the warm water. When all the flour is moist, add the butter bit by bit. When the last piece of butter has been added, increase the mixer speed to medium and knead the dough for 7 minutes. The dough should be elastic, but very tight and firm. If the dough seems too sticky, add more flour 1 tablespoon at a time, until the dough pulls away from the sides of the bowl.

Transfer the dough to a clean work surface and cover it with plastic wrap to keep it from drying out while you portion pieces. Divide the dough into walnut-size pieces (20 grams each if you have a scale), and arrange them on a couple of baking sheets; don't let the pieces touch. Cover the pans with plastic wrap and set them aside in a warm place to proof for about 1 hour.

When you are ready to start shaping the pretzels, first preheat the oven to 400 degrees F. Make a blanching solution by bringing the 10 cups of water and the baking soda to a boil in a large pot. (When choosing the pot, make sure the solution is at least 2½ inches deep.) The solution should be boiling when you start shaping the pretzels. Meanwhile, generously grease a baking sheet with oil or nonstick spray and set it aside. Make an egg wash by combining the egg with the 1 tablespoon water; whisk well, until all traces of the egg white have disappeared. Keep the egg wash in the refrigerator until ready to use.

To shape the pretzels, roll each little piece of dough into a 5- to 6-inch snake and tie it in a knot. Once you have rolled and tied 10 pretzels, immediately put them into the boiling solution. Boil each batch of pretzels for 30 seconds, dunking them underwater with a large spoon as they cook. After the 30 seconds, transfer the pretzels to a wire rack using a slotted spoon. Repeat this process until all the pretzels have been formed and boiled.

With the pretzels still on the wire rack, generously brush them with the egg wash, then transfer them to the well-greased baking sheet. Sprinkle the pretzels with the coarse sea salt and bake them for 20 minutes, rotating the pan after 10 minutes. If your oven has a convection fan, turn it on for the last 2 minutes of baking to increase browning.

Cool the pretzels on a wire rack. They are best eaten the day they are made, but you can store any leftovers in an airtight container.

MAKES ABOUT 5 DOZEN SMALL PRETZELS

PORTAGE BAY PANCAKES

Portage Bay Café owner, John Gunnar, shares this recipe for the restaurant's famous pancakes. For a heartier, nuttier flavor, you can use Bluebird Grain Farms' Whole Grain Emmer Flour instead of the soft white wheat variety. The amount of milk you add is up to you: add the full amount for thinner pancakes, less if you like them plump. If you can't find Bluebird's products, use a mixture of your favorite all-purpose and whole wheat flours.

1½ cups soft white wheat flour (preferably from Bluebird Grain Farms)

3 tablespoons sugar

1½ teaspoons baking powder

Pinch of sea salt

1 cup vanilla yogurt

2 large eggs

1 teaspoon vanilla extract

½ cup whole milk

3 tablespoons unsalted butter, for frying

In a large bowl, whisk the flour, sugar, baking powder, and salt to blend. In another bowl, whisk the yogurt, eggs, and vanilla until smooth. Pour the wet ingredients into the dry and gently whisk them together. Add about three-fourths of the milk, whisk gently, then add more milk to bring the batter to your desired consistency.

Heat a griddle or large nonstick frying pan over medium-low heat. Melt about ½ tablespoon of the butter and swirl to coat the bottom of the pan. When the foam subsides, ladle about ¼ cup of the batter into the pan for each pancake. When the pancakes have puffed and when bubbles begin to appear on the surface, about 3 minutes, flip them and continue cooking until the undersides are golden, another 1 to 2 minutes. Repeat with the remaining butter and batter.

Serve the pancakes with fresh fruit and maple syrup.

MAKES ABOUT 12 PANCAKES

ANIMAL PRODUCTS

Food is sustenance, and yet the path it takes to reach our table may be laden with hidden dangers, particularly in the case of meat and other animal products. The best way to ensure that you are getting the food you want is to travel the same path your food does. Countless studies have shown that the meat, milk, and eggs of healthy animals are more nutritious and safer to ingest than that of unhealthy ones.

Turnbow Flat Farm's cattle and chickens spend their lives grazing in (and fertilizing) Duncan and Mary MacDonald's front yard—a lush pasture on the rolling hillsides in the Palouse region—until just moments before slaughter. Beverly Phillips says that when she drinks fresh milk, she can taste the off flavors caused by stress on the animal, and so she raises her goats at Port Madison Farm with unwavering love and dedication. Her husband, Steve, makes, ages, and sells their cheeses himself. Like the Phillipses, Kurt Timmermeister makes his cheeses himself, on his farm, from milk supplied by his small herd of Jersey cows. He ages the cheeses in a cave he built under his cow pasture.

Pete Knutson and his son, Jonah, of Loki Fish Co. dress their wild, sustainably caught salmon at sea to maintain absolute freshness, and Pete has been an activist in marine conservation for decades. Taylor Shellfish Farms raises their renowned shellfish sustainably and is at the forefront of the movement to keep our waterways and beaches clean.

Respect for animals as living creatures and for the environment we all share were by far the most common themes among the farmers, ranchers, and fishermen I came to know. Their animals and their products provide us with nutritious, delicious food, and we can feel confident that by eating them we are not contributing to the detriment of their species or the planet.

PORT MADISON GOAT FARM AND DAIRY

— A Herd of Happy Goats —

In a corner of the barn, a dozen tiny kids tumble over one another in a playpen made of hay bales. In every combination of black and brown and white, they are a moving mass of spindly legs, wagging tails, and puppy bellies. One little tyke jams herself into a corner and presses with so much determination she manages to push the bales aside, and in a second, Beverly Phillips has scooped her up and cradles her. "Hi sweetie," she croons, and the kid calms immediately and gazes into Beverly's eyes.

The dozen active kids are the first wave born this year on Port Madison Farm on Bainbridge Island. They are three and four days old, and the ones that stay on the farm will consider themselves siblings and Beverly their mother. Beverly was there when they were born, she dried them off, and gave them their first bottle. She'll continue hand bottle-feeding them until they are weaned. Since Beverly is present at all the births, calls the dams' names as they deliver, and lets them lick her when she takes the kids, "Their reality is that she is their baby," Steve Phillips, Beverly's husband and Port Madison's cheesemaker, laughs while pointing to Beverly. "And the fact that she was also their mother doesn't seem to confuse them." As a result, the goats will always follow Beverly and behave for her.

Despite the complicated family tree, the goats are farm animals, and the realities of farm life are harsh. Goats average two to three kids per pregnancy. The Phillipses keep about one hundred goats, of which about sixty are bred each year. That means about one hundred fifty kids are born every spring; they will keep some, sell some for dairy or meat, and put some down.

Port Madison Farm's goats live a wonderful life. They are clean, well-fed, and bonded to humans, so they do not need to be herded by dogs. The Phillipses are proud of their goats' milk and the cheese they make from it, and they attribute much of their success to the way they manage their farm. Their dams, Steve says, "Have more babies with higher birth weights. They live longer. They give more milk." He adds that they don't lose dams in childbirth, they rarely have stillborn kids, and yet, he's not sure that economically it's a better way to do it than the way a lot of others do it. What Steve and Beverly do feel very strongly, however, is that their goats live stress-free lives that you can taste in the milk. The goats live with their siblings, their mothers, and their babies, and they come to be milked without being herded. Beverly explains that stress and adrenaline give an off-taste to milk, but you don't get any of that in theirs.

One hundred yards from the barn stands the Phillipses' house, a tall, New England–style farmhouse. Beverly had almost finished building it herself when she met Steve. She was raised in Maine, but moved to Bainbridge after a cross-country road trip in 1980 with her son. She did miss Maine just a little bit, and the farmhouse cured her. A software engineer, Beverly worked split shifts from home and spent the middle of every day working on the house, which sat on five acres not far from where she and her son lived in nearby Winslow.

In 1985, Beverly went on a trip to California with a friend. In Berkeley she met Steve, an industrial designer running a plastics factory. Six months later he joined her on Bainbridge Island. So how do a software engineer and an industrial designer get to be goat farmers? "Beverly made me an omelet with eggs that had come from range hens, and I realized I had never tasted real eggs before," Steve remembers. Within a month, they had over a hundred head of poultry. Beverly hoots with laughter, "I just wanted to be a subsistence farmer, I just wanted to grow my own food. But Steve always looks at things in a big way."

Steve bought chickens, ducks, turkeys, geese, pheasants, quails, and partridges. "Most people growing up in cities probably believe that it's impossible to make a living in agriculture. And there's certainly a lot of truth in it. Our society is not organizationally friendly to agriculture." But he didn't want to believe it. Beverly interrupts. "Let's just cut to the chase and say the poultry thing didn't work out." The slaughtering was daunting.

Meanwhile, the Phillipses were drowning in so much excess milk from the goats Beverly kept as pets that they'd started keeping pigs so it wouldn't go to waste. The milk was for personal use; Beverly drank it, and she had raised her son on it. But her pet goats had kids, and they had kids, and suddenly they had twelve goats and a lot of milk. Beverly remembers Steve telling her, "I don't want to live surrounded by goats. We have got to get rid of some of these goats." She said, "I can't do that, sorry. I guess we have to have a dairy."

The Phillipses built a barn that could house thirty goats, figuring they'd never have more than that. Their "foundation goat" was a dam named Eloise, and she produced two gallons of milk a day. The Phillipses raise purebred Nubians, which typically produce about 1,500 pounds of milk a year. On test, Eloise produced over 4,000 pounds. So when Steve did the math, he figured that with thirty goats like Eloise, they could make a very nice living. "And we certainly could have," Beverly smiles.

Then the Phillipses made a research trip to California, stopping at every goat dairy that would see them. Though the farms all raised heavy-producing Swiss breeds, they also all had a Nubian or two. When asked why, the farmers told them that's what they drank. "It turns out that Nubians have the richest, sweetest milk," Steve explains, "they just don't produce as much. So if you have a commercial herd and you're doing fluid milk, and you want to make money, then you can't raise Nubians."

But the Phillipses didn't know that yet. For several years, Beverly took care of the goats and Steve delivered milk all the way from Marysville down to Lacey. They sold lots of milk in the winter, but that meant breeding their goats year-round. Then they always had too much milk in the summer, because no one wanted it then—it seemed that everyone had a neighbor whose goat had just given birth and was giving away milk for free—so they watered tomatoes with the milk, fed it to their pigs, and started making cheese.

Although it was Beverly who began making small batches (just two gallons at a time in her kitchen), and then bought a pasteurizer so she

could make it to sell, it was Steve who eventually got hooked. He took a Washington State University cheesemaking class in Pullman, and then, says Beverly, there was a lot of trial and error, and a lot of cheese got fed to the pigs.

Compared to the creameries Steve visited with WSU, theirs was "a little doll-house version," as Beverly describes it. When they decided to invest in cheesemaking equipment, one of the big challenges was to figure out the scale of operation they wanted. They had decided that their ideal goat population was one hundred, and they would just do cheese, not fluid milk.

With their cheesemaking future decided, Steve embraced it in his typical fashion. Beverly tells with wonder, "He just bought two plane tickets and took his daughter to Paris. He went to a cheese shop and said, 'I am a cheesemaker from America. Who can I talk to?'" Steve knew no one there, spoke only a little high-school French, and had spent three months teaching himself cheese vocabulary. The shopkeeper introduced him to a cheesemaker in the Loire Valley, and they hopped on a train to meet him. Less than two weeks later Steve was home. He had met twenty small cheesemakers all over France, working in "enormously efficient small dairies where every detail had been worked out over centuries."

Steve compares making cheese to sailing. You can't go from here to there in a straight line, and must take into account the wind and tide and make adjustments. The farm's milk changes as the seasons change, as the goats' diet changes, and as the kids mature, so the recipes and techniques must change, too. Steve makes yogurt all year except when the goats aren't producing, and has a diverse list of cheeses including spring cheese, cheddar, blue, a Brie-style, and both fresh and aged chèvre, but he decides day to day what to work on. Every day Beverly milks the goats twice, and every day Steve makes, checks, and tastes their cheeses to decide what's ready to be salted, turned, aged, or sold.

Then Steve catches the ferry from Bainbridge Island with coolers full of cheese to sell at farmers markets in Seattle. There are distributors who would take his cheese, saving him time and the ferry commute, but he is adamant: "Quality control. If you're doing it yourself, you care. You want people to get it as fresh as possible, in as good condition as possible. We're putting our name on it." And the closer he is to his customers, Steve says, the happier he is. "I like the people. You're selling to people who are the kind of people who get up on a Saturday morning and go to a farmers market to get something nice for somebody they love. I just can't think of anybody I'd rather do business with."

As dairy farmers, Steve and Beverly are on call 24/7. Steve notes that this is news to a lot of people who think dairy farming sounds like fun. He admits that even they didn't really know what they were getting themselves into. "No one knows. No one would do it if they knew," Beverly says. "It's sort of like having children," Steve adds. "You wouldn't do it if you knew how much work it was."

Married for twenty-two years, the Phillipses have yet to take a honeymoon. And they realize that one day they'll have to retire. They talk about it, Steve says. "But it's not going to happen," Beverly finishes.

GOAT CHEESECAKE WITH
PEARS AND HONEY

This rich, creamy cheesecake from Chef Charlie Durham of Hudson Public House in Seattle is just barely sweet enough to make fans of sweet desserts happy, but savory enough to satisfy those who'd rather end their meal with a cheese course. Don't skip the garnishes—the honey drizzle brings out the subtle honey flavor of the cheesecake and balances the tangy goat cheese, and the pear adds a bright, juicy freshness to the dessert. Be sure to use your favorite local honey and perfectly ripe local pears to ensure this is an unforgettable dessert.

1 cup pine nuts

1 cup fresh breadcrumbs

3 tablespoons sugar

1 tablespoon plus 1½ teaspoons all-purpose flour

Pinch of salt

¼ cup (½ stick) unsalted butter, melted

2 pounds cream cheese, at room temperature

11 ounces goat cheese, at room temperature

¾ cup honey, plus more for drizzling

2 large eggs

1 cup sour cream

Juice of 1 lime (about 1½ tablespoons)

3 to 4 firm but ripe pears

Preheat the oven to 350 degrees F. Butter or spray a 10-inch springform pan and set aside.

Heat a small heavy skillet over medium-low heat. Add the pine nuts and slowly toast them, stirring constantly, until pale golden, about 5 minutes, then set aside to cool. Put the breadcrumbs, sugar, flour, salt, and cooled pine nuts into the bowl of a food processor and pulse until the nuts are coarsely chopped. Add the melted butter and pulse to blend. Press the mixture into the bottom of the prepared pan, working the crumbs into the inner edge of the pan so that there is no gap between the bottom and sides of the pan. Bake until lightly browned, about 15 minutes. Set aside to cool.

In the bowl of an electric mixer on medium speed, cream together the cream cheese and goat cheese until smooth. Add the honey and mix until blended. Scrape the sides of the bowl, then using the lowest speed, add the eggs one at a time, mixing each until it is fully incorporated into the cream cheese mixture. Scrape the bowl again and then add the sour cream and lime juice and mix just until the sour cream is incorporated and the mixture is very smooth. Pour the batter into the cooled pan and bake until it is set and pale golden just around the edges, about 1 hour. Allow the cheesecake to cool at room temperature, then chill it completely in the refrigerator before slicing.

Right before serving, cut just enough pears into ½-inch dice to make about ¼ cup topping for each slice of cheesecake. Serve with a generous drizzle of honey.

MAKES 12 TO 14 SERVINGS

BRUSCHETTA OF GOAT BRIE
AND TOMATO JAM

Chef Walter Pisano uses Port Madison Farm's goat brie for this striking hors d'oeuvre at his restaurant, Tulio. A dollop of bright scarlet jam tops the warm, creamy white cheese as it oozes over a crusty slice of baguette. It's an edible work of art.

½ teaspoon chili flakes

3 whole allspice berries

2 whole cloves

1½ pounds ripe tomatoes, peeled, seeded, and diced

½ cup sugar

¼ cup apple cider vinegar

1 teaspoon sea salt

1 artisan-style crusty baguette

Extra-virgin olive oil, for brushing the bread slices (about ⅓ cup)

Sea salt and freshly ground black pepper

8 ounces goat brie cheese

First, make the tomato jam. Prepare a sachet of spices by cutting a 4- to 5-inch square of cheesecloth. Place the chili flakes, allspice berries, and cloves in the center, draw the sides up around the spices to make a little bag and tie it securely closed with kitchen string. In a heavy-bottomed saucepan slowly bring the tomatoes, sugar, vinegar, salt, and the sachet of spices to a boil. Reduce the heat to low and simmer, stirring frequently, for about 30 minutes, or until the mixture is thick and has a jam-like consistency. Remove from the heat and discard the sachet. Cool in the refrigerator.

To serve, preheat the broiler. Slice the baguette into 16 slices about ½ inch thick, then brush both sides of each slice with a little of the olive oil and sprinkle with salt and pepper. Lay the slices on a baking sheet and broil the bread on one side just until the edges are golden, 2 to 3 minutes. Meanwhile, cut the cheese into 16 thin wedges. Remove the bread slices from the oven, turn them over and top each with a wedge of cheese. Broil for another 30 seconds to soften the cheese. Transfer the toasts to a platter and garnish each with a rounded teaspoon of tomato jam and a few drops of extra-virgin olive oil. Season to taste with a little more fresh black pepper and serve right away.

MAKES 16 TOASTS FOR 8 SERVINGS

KURTWOOD FARMS

Becoming the Source

Dinah 2.0 moves in slow motion, with much effort. She's trying to follow Kurt Timmermeister, Kurtwood Farms' owner/farmer/cheesemaker, and she's obviously moving as fast as she can. Her belly is huge; a calf's due within days. She doesn't just moo at Kurt, she bellows. She's lonely, he says. She wants to be with her girlfriends in the pasture, but Kurt wants her safely in the barn when she delivers.

Out in the pasture there's Andi, the first cow born on the farm to come into milk, and her son, a young steer named Teddy; Lily; Boo and her new calf, Fleuracita; Luna, Dinah's one-year-old daughter; and a bull called Joe. There are also pigs, chickens, dogs, and plenty of vegetables on Kurtwood Farms' 13 acres, but this little herd of Jersey cows includes the producers of the rich, creamy milk Kurt uses to make Dinah's Cheese. A mild, buttery, mold-ripened Camembert-style cheese, it is the latest success on Kurt's incredibly varied resume. He is a farmer, author, chef, restaurateur, and cheesemaker.

A Seattle native, Kurt started in the restaurant business in the kitchen at Pike Place Market's Maximilien Restaurant. His resume includes every memorable Seattle restaurant from the early '80s; among them Chez Shea, Fullers, the Brasserie, and the Columbia Tower Club. When he first opened Cafe Septieme, it was just a little coffee shop and bakery. As business grew, he expanded to larger and larger spaces. He'd bought a house and a few acres on Vashon Island because it was affordable. He was a city kid (he vaguely remembers seeing a cow on a school trip in the third grade), who just happened to live in the country. "It was a long way to go to work. But I didn't really think about it too much. Vashon was still off the map. So it was really cheap. And I moved into this chicken house and I thought it was so beautiful, but it was a dump on a crappy piece of land. I didn't know what I was going to do, but somehow I was drawn to this."

When he's asked why he made the switch from city life, Kurt says he doesn't know, despite having written a truly compelling book called *Growing a Farmer: How I Learned to Live Off the Land*. "It's hard to put a finger on it," he says, "I wanted to do it, so I did it."

Kurt seemed to forget everything he learned running Cafe Septieme the moment he put on his farmer's cap. "I met someone who was selling vegetables. And I was like, 'Let's sell vegetables. We'll have a vegetable farm. I can do this.' And it was a disaster. Not a complete disaster, but pretty close." It was hard work, even harder than Kurt expected, which says a lot, considering his crazy working hours at Septieme, spending every weekend and holiday standing behind the bar watching his friends, family, and customers lead their lives. The soil was poor, and Kurt admits, "I wasn't particularly good at it."

Kurt's original log farmhouse is coffee-table-book beautiful, but it had neither a kitchen nor a bathroom. Over time, he restored the home, and today it is probably the loveliest log cabin imaginable. Kurt feels a great sense of responsibility living in his old house, so rather than ripping into its walls for plumbing, he had a separate building designed to house a large kitchen, dining room, and bathroom, financing it with the money from the sale of Cafe Septieme.

While still in the design phase and trying to figure out how he was going to make a living without the café, Kurt took a trip to Portland, Oregon. He had dinner at Michael Hebb's underground supper club, Ripe, which was unusually located in the middle of an industrial area. It got him thinking: If he built a really big kitchen and held family-style dinners once a week and charged a flat rate, would anyone come? "I can do that," he thought, and so he built his kitchen for a crowd.

Then Kurt wrote a 250-word email. It went to thirty people, mostly friends and customers who'd bought vegetables from him. And by the next day the first five weeks were full. Within a year the mailing list had grown to five hundred and Kurt had found himself a part-time job to support his farm. "I cooked; I made the bread, the cheese, things like pâtés, pickles, jams; I always made the dessert, everything that could be done ahead of time." And then his chef for the day (up-and-comers like Tyler Palagi from Spring Hill) came from Seattle, at seven or eight in the morning. Kurt put out produce and meat from his farm, and they spent the day cooking what he'd given them. He held the dinners year-round, although summer was crazy, with twice as many requests as he could fill, while winter was a hard sell.

Though he'd wanted to be a farmer, now he was right back in the restaurant business. Then he met a farmer with a Holstein who was selling raw milk for eight dollars per gallon. Kurt thought, "Eight dollars per gallon! I'm going to be rich!" and bought himself a cow. "She was

not a good purchase. But she was the first one, and her name was Dinah. I started selling raw milk. I milked her by hand. I didn't know anything. I certainly didn't follow current protocol for raw milk at all. And somehow it didn't cross my mind. We had this sort of collective culture of, 'the government is out to get us and the government is wrong and obviously we're good people and we went to college and those cows are healthy.' The fact that I knew nothing about cows somehow was never in the discussion. So I did it for a couple of years. And thankfully, no one ever got sick. And it was beautiful milk."

Then one day Kurt heard a story on the radio about a farm in Vancouver, Washington, selling raw milk without a license to people in Portland. A number of children had gotten sick from *E. coli.* "I thought, 'Oh my God, oh my God, what do I do!' And I literally went out and unplugged my farm stand and told all my customers, 'I'm not selling any more milk.'"

He applied for a license from the Washington State Department of Agriculture. "And as it turns out, they are not out to get you!" Kurt got a Grade A license, raised his price to ten dollars a gallon, and just broke even. The tough part, he says, is not selling milk. It's getting the cows bred and making sure that they are always producing. Before he learned to cut his pastures better and get rid of cows that didn't breed or produce well, Kurt remembers watching his cows "just chewing up food, all day long."

Then Dinah tested positive for a disease called Q fever. The test didn't mean she had it, or that her milk was bad, but it meant she had to be destroyed. Kurt made a fuss, and shortly after that, inspectors showed up to test for *Listeria.* They found nothing, but Kurt was exhausted. "I didn't want to fight anymore. I knew I was going to lose. I wasn't making any

money. But I had a half dozen cows by this time. And I really liked them. The pastures were looking good. I knew I had to do something." That's when he suddenly realized, "I'll make cheese!"

"My great strength at this point," Kurt says with a shrug, "is that I've done enough stuff that I know that I'm competent. It's like a leap of faith. I'll figure it out." So Kurt searched for and found a small bulk tank for chilling the milk and a small pasteurizer, importing them from Slovenia and the Netherlands, where cheese is still made on small farms.

Kurt practiced with four gallons on the stove at a time. Fortunately for him, the style of cheese he makes gets eaten young—he only had to wait twenty-five days to know that the first batches were bad. "I had never used a cheese vat before. I had never seen one. And there are instructions with it, but they assume you know how to make cheese. I did something wrong the first couple of times and the guy in the Netherlands says, 'You actually need to put the milk in first.' And I'm like, 'Yeah, I knew that.'"

Kurt made a new batch every three days. He'd chosen a very fussy cheese to make.

Getting the bloom to grow completely and quickly, not to mention white with no holes in it, is a factor of temperature, humidity, salinity, and acid level. There were batches of what he called "not-salty things with no mold" and "bald and spotty batches," and the pigs at Kurtwood Farms ate hundreds of pounds of bad cheese. But slowly things improved until it became a truly lovely, lily-white, buttery cheese that ripens evenly, and smells of fresh cream with just a hint of salt.

Kurt named it Dinah's Cheese because it's not French. "It's not Fromage de Vashon. It's about this place, and this island, but it's not something we do traditionally, so it can't be called Vashon. This is a farmstead cheese. I personally and physically go out there and milk the cows twice a day and make that cheese every three days. It's very hands-on, and that's what I want to convey. It takes me twenty-five days to make this cheese. From milk from a cow that was born here two and a half years ago, that I bred a year ago, on a farm I started fifteen years ago. That's what goes into making Dinah's Cheese."

DINAH'S CHEESE WITH CARAWAY ONIONS

This finger-licking appetizer from Chef Mark Fuller at Spring Hill is reminiscent of the best French onion soup: sweet pan-roasted onions and buttery melted cheese on crunchy baguette. At the restaurant, Chef Fuller serves each toast topped with a bright salad of parsley and frisée with house-pickled green garlic, sauced with a rich red wine–fortified beef jus.

¼ cup canola oil

2 large yellow onions, halved, peeled, and thinly sliced into half moons

Kosher salt

1 teaspoon caraway seed

1 artisan-style crusty baguette

Clarified butter or extra-virgin olive oil, for brushing the bread (about ⅓ cup)

1 round of Dinah's Cheese (8 ounces)

Heat the canola oil in a medium-sized heavy-bottomed pot over high heat, add the onions, and stir to coat. Add about 1 teaspoon kosher salt (to leach the water from the onions), and stir to mix. Cook, stirring constantly, until the liquid evaporates, about 5 minutes. Reduce the heat to medium and slowly caramelize the onions, stirring occasionally, until they turn a deep brown color, about 30 minutes. As they start to brown you'll need to stir more frequently (or reduce the heat) so that they don't burn. Add salt to taste.

While the onions are cooking, heat a small skillet over medium heat. Add the caraway seeds and lightly toast them, shaking the pan, about 1 minute. When they are cool, grind them and mix the powdered caraway into the caramelized onions. Cover the pan to keep the onions warm.

To make the toast, preheat the oven to 400 degrees F. Slice the baguette on a severe angle into long slices ½ inch thick. Brush both sides with a little olive oil or clarified butter and spread them out on a baking sheet. Toast them in the oven until golden, then flip them over and toast the other side (about 2 minutes per side). Remove the toasts, but leave the oven on.

To serve, spread 2 tablespoons of the onions onto each slice of baguette. Cut Dinah's cheese into 6 wedges. Carefully slice each wedge lengthwise and lay the two pieces over the onion on each toast. Put the pan of toasts in the oven for just long enough to soften the cheese, then serve right away.

MAKES 12 TOASTS FOR 6 SERVINGS

TURNBOW FLAT FARM

Something Old, Something New

Like a scene in a snow globe, big fluffy snowflakes gently drift down in front of the brick-red-painted farmhouse with its long covered porch and gray roof. Forty acres of snow-covered pasture stretches to the west, rising to the crest of the next butte. Although it may look like a postcard of an old farm in the undulating landscape around Palouse, Washington, the house is actually brand-new, and the pasture, though shallow-soiled, is lush in the growing season. Like everything at Turnbow Flat Farm, this pastoral scene is a seamless combination of old and new.

This is where Mary and Duncan MacDonald live with their young daughter, Lida, and an ebullient Weimaraner named Otis. Mary is the sixth generation of her family to farm this land, and Lida will be the seventh to grow up here. Their farmhouse sits on five acres they received as a wedding present from Mary's parents, Janet and Ben Barstow, who live in the original farmhouse less than five minutes away.

Janet's great-great-grandfather Benjamin Riley Turnbow and his family came from Iowa in the 1870s to homestead this land. Their 1880 deed is framed and hangs on the wall of the Barstows' living room, alongside sepia-toned photos of serious-looking Turnbow men and old Palouse.

Growing up on the farm, money was always tight. Mary's father told her that "anything you want to do, anything at all, if it involves agriculture, you're not going to make any money, but you will never meet nicer people." Still, she knew that she'd want to be involved in some

way, and earned degrees from the University of Idaho in crop science and agriculture communication. She studied abroad in Taiwan, where she learned to grow exotic crops like dragon fruit, papaya, and mango, and taught about growing wheat on thousand-acre farms. When she returned, she took a job at the Pullman Chamber of Commerce as the director of the Lentil Festival. "Not *a* lentil festival," she explains with a grin, "*the* lentil festival."

Mary radiates energy, laughs easily, and communicates the passion she feels for her livelihood and lifestyle with such intelligence and composure, it's clear there's more to the lentil festival than just lentils. Working late one Saturday, she decided to have a drink with friends in downtown Pullman. And that's when she met Duncan.

Duncan grew up in Louisiana, where he earned his BA in accounting at Louisiana State University, then went to law school. After earning his JD he moved to Whitefish, Montana, to ski, but ended up running a web marketing business until he realized that he hardly had time to ski anymore. He moved to Seattle and took a job with Microsoft. Ten years later, Duncan realized that if he wanted a family, he'd better start soon, and he wanted his children to have the kind of rural childhood that he'd had.

Both of Duncan's brothers had moved to Seattle, so he didn't want to go too far. After looking at Spokane and Winthrop, he leaned toward Pullman. He brought his brothers and mother for a weekend to show them around, and that's when he met Mary. Two months later he moved to Pullman, and the following summer they were married in the barn her great-great-grandfather built. Duncan wore flip-flops and khakis.

"Farming wasn't a natural career choice in any way," Duncan readily admits, "as much as it was an evolution." Food had always been an important part of his life growing up in Louisiana. "It's a very celebratory culture," he wryly explains. As he learned more about processed food and how the rest of the world eats compared to most of America, he realized that he'd like to have more control over what he ate, and that he'd like to raise some of his food himself. The first time he ate farm-fresh eggs at the Barstows', he couldn't believe how different they were from the eggs he bought at the grocery store. That's what really woke him up, and he thought, "This is real food." Never one to back down from a challenge, he and Mary talked about eating less processed food, raised in more humane ways, and as they did, they became more interested in raising it for other people too. "If we're going to raise one pig, we might as well raise twenty."

At first Mary kept her job at the Chamber, and Duncan worked remotely for Microsoft. He read everything about farming that he could get his hands on. His copy of *Black's Law Dictionary* shares a shelf with the *Merck Veterinary Manual* and *The Complete Book of Composting*. Soon Duncan left Microsoft to spend a year apprenticing with a local farmer. He read a lot of Michael Pollan, who writes about how eating real food is good for us and good for the environment, and Joel Salatin at Polyface Farms. He was intrigued by Polyface's amazing productivity on a relatively small farm, and how they managed to keep improving their land, rather than degrading it.

Today the MacDonalds raise cattle, pigs, chickens (some for laying and some for meat), and turkeys, and soon they'll add sheep and possibly goats. Duncan says he has a black thumb and can't plant anything, but he loves the dynamics of working with animals, particularly the intersection of species—when you put different animals together, you can take better care of your land, better care of your animals, and have profitability on a smaller scale. This is how farms used to work one hundred years ago, including theirs. Records show that in 1889 the Turnbows raised wheat, oats, cows, pigs, horses, and chickens. Today Ben and Janet grow wheat, barley, peas, some lentils, and some hay. Thanks to Duncan and Mary, Turnbow Flat Farm is once again diversified. "We just added the livestock portion back to it. We're not taking anything out of production," Mary explains, "we're using ground that's too wet or too steep to farm grains, and just using the land more efficiently."

But they still had a lot to learn. Their multispecies model meant they needed to be experts on pigs, cows, and different kinds of poultry, and they also needed to know how to process them all. Mary sums it up: "It was an adventure."

In nature, animals group tightly and move frequently for protection, so the land gets to rest and recover. The MacDonalds mimic nature by dividing their pasture into strips. Each species of animal eats the pasture differently, and by rotating the animals through the strips and allowing the strips to rest before they are eaten again, the land is actually healthier with the animals than without them. When cattle are confined to a smaller area, they will theoretically take one bite of

every blade of grass before moving on the next day. The chickens come through next, eating different grasses than the cows do, as well as the bugs and grubs from the ground, and they spread out the manure the cows left behind. When the cows come back, the pasture is clean. Grass that's given time to heal puts roots deeper, increasing its water-holding capacity and getting more nutrients down farther in the soil. The system also increases the diversity of the grasses because the animals eat a little of everything, then drop the seeds in the next section of pasture.

Their animals end up as meat, but until then, their lives are idyllic. Pigs roll in the mud and dig holes, cows raise their own calves and graze together in the lush pasture, taking turns with the chickens. Mary shows me Mona and Lisa, two Piedmontese heifers, pure white, with small ears. "Don't they look like teddy bears?" she asks. Mary grew up taking care of animals, and always understood that "as much as you love this animal, you also love steak, so keep that in mind." For Duncan there was more of a learning curve. Even before moving to Pullman, he watched the Barstows process a cow. "It was hard," he says, suddenly serious, with the same intense energy that Mary has. "I'd never really seen a lot of things die. I can't say that any part of me enjoyed it, but I was okay with the way the animal lived, and the way the animal died, and I thought that if I can't be part of this, then I don't have any business being a meat eater."

Mary and Duncan started their lives together and their farm at the same time. "We believe very much in sustainability," says Mary. "And for us," adds Duncan, "it's a combination of lifestyle, economics, and environmental sustainability. We had to find a way to do this where it made sense financially, we enjoyed it, and we could do it without trashing the land around us." They sell only through direct marketing so they can gate it and stay small, ensuring they stick to their quality goals. They are proud of the excellent flavor and quality of their meat, and have made a commitment to their community by selling locally, offering farm tours, supporting local businesses, composting diligently, and acting as good stewards of the land.

Even on a snowy day, the farm is growing. We're outside watching a very pregnant chocolate-brown cow with a thick, heavy coat standing quietly under a monumental oak tree in front of the old barn. She's motionless in the absolute quiet as huge snowflakes collect on her back. Everyone is excited because her calf will be the first of the season. The farm is changing, but if old Benjamin Riley Turnbow looks down, he'll recognize it for sure.

ASIAN BEEF SATAY

At Lisbet and Ron Mielke's restaurant, Ravish, on Eastlake Avenue in Seattle, Chef Kelly Daly serves a variety of small plates that are perfect for sharing, like these Thai-inspired skewers. Serve them to a crowd as an appetizer, or with rice and grilled vegetables to make a meal. Both the marinade and dipping sauce work equally well with chicken or pork, and the marinade also makes a terrific dressing for salad or mixed vegetables.

1 bunch fresh cilantro

¼ cup peeled, coarsely chopped fresh ginger

6 to 8 cloves garlic

⅓ cup light brown sugar

1 tablespoon ground cumin

2 teaspoons red pepper flakes

½ cup fresh lime juice (about 2 medium limes), plus lime wedges for serving

¼ cup soy sauce

1 cup canola or olive oil

2 pounds beef flank steak, sirloin, or tri-tip

Dipping Sauce

½ cup canned unsweetened coconut milk

½ cup plus 2 tablespoons fresh orange juice (1 to 2 medium oranges), divided

¾ teaspoon Thai yellow curry paste

1½ teaspoons light brown sugar

1½ teaspoons cornstarch

Pick the cilantro leaves from the stems, saving a few whole sprigs for garnish. In a food processor, purée the cilantro leaves, ginger, garlic, brown sugar, cumin, and pepper flakes to form a paste. Add the lime juice and soy sauce and pulse to blend. Slowly add the oil and process until the marinade is smooth.

If using flank steak, slice the meat across the grain on the diagonal into long ½-inch-thick slices. If using sirloin or tri-tip, cut the meat into ¾- to 1-inch cubes. Put the meat into a large bowl and pour the marinade over it. Gently mix, making sure the marinade coats all sides. Cover the bowl and let the meat marinate for at least 2 hours (and up to 24 hours) in the refrigerator (or freeze for up to 1 month before continuing).

Next, make the dipping sauce. In a saucepan over medium heat, combine the coconut milk, ½ cup of the orange juice, curry paste, and brown sugar and simmer for 3 to 4 minutes. Whisk the cornstarch into the remaining 2 tablespoons of orange juice, and then whisk the mixture into the saucepan. Reduce the heat to low and simmer, whisking often, until the sauce thickens, about 5 minutes. Set aside to cool.

At least 30 minutes before you need them, soak about 18 (for flank steak) or 12 (for cubed meat) bamboo skewers in a shallow pan of water for at least 30 minutes. (This will help prevent the wood from burning on the grill.) Make sure they're submerged. When you're ready to proceed, thread the meat onto the skewers. Grill to desired doneness and transfer to a large platter. Garnish with the fresh lime wedges and reserved cilantro sprigs, and serve with the dipping sauce.

MAKES 4 TO 6 MAIN COURSE SERVINGS, OR 12 SERVINGS AS AN APPETIZER

PASTA KIMA

Chef Nick Pitsilionis grew up working in his family's Italian restaurant in Alaska and spending his summers in Greece. When he opened his restaurant, The Black Cypress, in Pullman, he wanted a place like the mountain tavernas he frequented in his family's Greek village. They serve "very simple, ultra-seasonal, local food," and so does Nick. He grows much of his restaurant's produce at his own farm and works with nearby farmers who raise the rest. This sauce, explains Nick, is the workhorse behind many better-known Greek dishes including Pastitsio and Moussaka. It may read like a lot of garlic and thyme, but trust him—the long, slow cooking brings all the flavors together to make a truly harmonious and memorable dish.

½ teaspoon whole black peppercorns

½ teaspoon whole allspice berries

¼ cup white wine

3 bay leaves

1 cinnamon stick, about 2 inches long

¼ teaspoon red pepper flakes, plus more as desired

One 28-ounce can whole peeled plum tomatoes

4 tablespoons vegetable oil, divided

2½ cups finely diced yellow onion

½ cup finely minced garlic (about 15 cloves)

12 ounces ground pork

1 pound ground beef

¾ ounce fresh thyme sprigs (one typical package)

1 pound dry pasta, preferably bucatini

Extra-virgin olive oil, for drizzling

1½ ounces Myzithra cheese, grated (about ½ cup)

Kosher salt

Sugar

Put the peppercorns and allspice in a small, heavy-duty resealable plastic bag and use the back of a skillet or the smooth side of a meat mallet to coarsely crack them. (Alternatively, use a mortar and pestle.) Put them in a small saucepot with the wine, bay leaves, cinnamon stick, and red pepper flakes; bring to a simmer over low heat.

Drain the can of tomatoes in a colander over a bowl. Pour the accumulated liquid into the pot with the simmering wine and spices and continue to cook on low heat to soften the spices. Crush the tomato flesh by squeezing it in your hand and set it aside.

Add 2 tablespoons of the vegetable oil to a large heavy-bottomed pot over medium heat. Add half of the onions and cook, stirring often, until they are soft, translucent, and beginning to caramelize and turn golden, about 5 minutes. Add the remaining 2 tablespoons vegetable oil, the remaining onions and the garlic, and cook, stirring constantly, until they begin to soften, 1 to 2 minutes more.

Add the pork, breaking it up with the back of a spoon. Stir often and cook until the meat is brown and all of the onions have begun to caramelize, about 5 more minutes. Add the beef, use the back of a spoon to break it up, and cook until browned, stirring constantly. When the meat has cooked through, add the wine and spice mixture and stir well to blend. Add the crushed tomatoes and any liquid that has accumulated, stir to incorporate, then cover the pot, reduce the heat to low, and simmer gently for 30 minutes, stirring occasionally. Use kitchen string to tie the thyme into 2 or 3 bundles, then add them to the pot. Stir to combine; cover the pot and continue to cook gently for another 30 minutes.

About 15 minutes before the sauce is ready, bring a large pot of salted water to a boil and cook the pasta according to package instructions. Drain well, drizzle with a couple tablespoons of extra-virgin olive oil, add the cheese, toss to coat, and set the pasta aside momentarily.

Remove the thyme bundles, bay leaves, and cinnamon stick from the sauce. Add salt and sugar to taste (start with about 1½ teaspoons of salt and about 1 teaspoon of sugar).

To serve, divide the pasta onto large flat plates, spreading it out so that there's plenty of surface area to cover with sauce. Ladle the sauce over and serve right away.

MAKES 6 SERVINGS

WHOLE ROASTED CHICKEN WITH PEACHES, ANISE HYSSOP, AND HAZELNUTS

Matt Dillon, chef and owner of The Corson Building and Sitka & Spruce, raises chickens at The Corson Building for their eggs, but he gets the chickens he cooks from Stokesberry Sustainable Farms. This juicy roast screams summer as it drips with nutty, buttery goodness and warm peach juices, so be sure to use "ripe, beautiful, naturally raised, loving peaches," advises Matt. Anise hyssop leaves look like mint (and are part of the mint family), but they taste and smell like anise. The tender leaves are delicious with the peaches, and the bright flavor is a lovely counterpoint to the rich drippings.

Brine

8 cups water

½ cup sugar

½ cup kosher salt

1 lemon, sliced

1 head of garlic, cut in half crosswise

30 peppercorns

Chicken

1 whole chicken (about 3 pounds)

¾ cup (1½ sticks) plus 5 tablespoons unsalted butter, at room temperature

1 lemon, zested and juiced (about 2 teaspoons zest and 3 tablespoons juice)

1 tablespoon chopped fresh thyme

1 tablespoon chopped fresh marjoram

1 teaspoon minced garlic

1 teaspoon minced shallot

¾ teaspoon kosher salt

¼ teaspoon freshly ground black pepper

2 tablespoons olive oil

½ cup roughly chopped toasted hazelnuts

2 whole peaches, halved to remove the pits, then each half cut into thirds

15 medium anise hyssop leaves (or substitute mint)

The day before serving, make a brine by bringing the water, sugar, salt, lemon, garlic, and peppercorns to a boil in a large pot. Stir to dissolve the sugar and salt. Let the brine cool to room temperature and then chill it in the refrigerator. When the brine is cold, add the chicken, making sure it is fully submerged (you can cover it with a piece of parchment and weigh it down with a lid smaller then the pot). Leave the chicken in the brine overnight (up to 24 hours) in the refrigerator.

Put ¾ cup of the butter into a medium bowl; add the lemon zest, thyme, marjoram, garlic, shallot, and the salt and pepper. Combine by using a rubber spatula to smooth and work the butter with the rest of the ingredients until they are well blended.

Preheat the oven to 400 degrees F. Rinse and dry the chicken. Place the chicken breast-side up on your work surface; beginning at the large cavity near the tail, use your fingers to very carefully separate, but not tear or remove, the skin from the meat. Carefully stuff the flavored butter under the skin of the chicken, all the way into the pocket you created, getting it in and around the legs and breasts. Truss the chicken with butcher twine and place it on a baking sheet. Brush the chicken all over with the olive oil and season it with salt and pepper. Roast until the temperature between the body and thigh reaches 155 degrees F, about 1 hour. Remove the chicken from the oven and allow it to rest, covered loosely with foil. It will continue cooking a little as it rests and will release some of its juices. Save these juices.

While the chicken rests, heat the remaining 5 tablespoons butter in a sauté pan over medium heat until the butter foams, smells nutty, and turns a pale golden color. Remove it from the heat and add the hazelnuts, lemon juice, and resting juices. Season to taste with more salt and pepper.

To serve, cut the chicken into 2 drumsticks, 2 thighs, and 2 breasts, and then cut the breasts in half widthwise. Arrange the pieces on a platter, tucking the peach slices and anise hyssop leaves "in a tangled dance of goodness." Drizzle the butter sauce all over.

MAKES 4 SERVINGS

PASTURED CHICKEN WITH NORTHWEST PORTER AND MORELS

This hearty, full-flavored dish from Chef Keith Luce, formerly of The Herbfarm (now at his own Luce & Hawkins in Jamesport, NY), comes together easily and then braises for about 45 minutes, making it a perfect family supper. But the rich, heady sauce studded with luxurious morels lets it do double-duty as the main course for a dinner party, too. Serve it with rice, mashed potatoes, or crusty bread so that no sauce goes to waste.

1 ounce dried morels

¼ cup all-purpose flour

⅛ teaspoon ground cloves

⅛ teaspoon ground juniper berries

¼ teaspoon ground allspice

1 naturally raised and pastured chicken (about 5 pounds), cut into 8 pieces

Sea salt and white pepper

1 tablespoon grapeseed oil (or substitute canola oil)

¼ cup (½ stick) unsalted butter, cut into several pieces

1 small yellow onion, finely chopped

1 cup of your favorite micro-brewed porter or stout beer

¼ cup crème fraiche

1 teaspoon champagne or sherry vinegar

¼ cup chopped Italian parsley

1 tablespoon chopped chives or shallots

Freshly ground black pepper

Swish the dried morels in a large bowl of water and drain them. Put them into a medium bowl and add 1½ cups very hot water; set aside to reconstitute for about 20 minutes. Lift the morels from the water, leaving any sand or grit behind. Reserve the soaking liquid.

While the morels are softening, stir together the flour, cloves, juniper, and allspice. Generously season both sides of the chicken pieces with salt and white pepper, then dredge them in the flour and spice mixture.

Warm a large sauté or roasting pan (large enough to accommodate all of the chicken pieces without crowding—or, use a smaller pan and brown in two batches) over medium heat. Add the grapeseed oil and then add the chicken pieces, skin side down. Once all the chicken is in the pan and the pan has heated up again enough to sizzle the chicken, add the butter pieces, distributing them evenly in the pan. Brown the chicken thoroughly, about 6 minutes (the pan should not be too hot), then turn the pieces over and brown the other side, about 5 minutes more. Remove the chicken from the pan and pat with a paper towel to remove excess oil.

Add the chopped onion to the hot pan and cook until softened, about 3 minutes, then deglaze the pan by adding the reserved mushroom water (pour slowly so that any grit from the mushrooms remains in the bottom of the bowl). Scrape the bottom of the pan to loosen any bits that may be stuck to it. Simmer, reducing the liquid to a syrupy consistency, about 4 minutes. Add the beer, bring to a boil, and then add the morels. Add the chicken pieces, being sure to nestle them into the mushrooms and liquid. Bring the mixture to a boil, reduce the heat to low, then cover and simmer gently for 30 to 45 minutes, or until the chicken is very tender. Turn the pieces from time to time, removing them as they are ready. The breasts will likely be cooked before the other parts have finished. As you remove the pieces, place them in a pan or on a plate and cover to keep warm.

Bring the liquid in the pan back to a boil. Next, you will add the crème fraiche—but instead of adding it directly into the hot liquid, you must "temper" it so that it doesn't break or curdle. First, put the crème fraiche into a small mixing bowl, then slowly whisk in a few tablespoons of the hot liquid. Continue until you've gradually added in about 1 cup of the liquid. Add this back into the pan, whisking constantly, and reduce the heat to a simmer. Whisk in the vinegar, then taste and adjust the seasoning. Add the chicken back to the pan and gently baste it with the sauce until it is well coated and the chicken has warmed through.

Garnish with the chopped parsley and chives and a grind of black pepper.

MAKES 4 SERVINGS

MOROCCAN SPICED LAMB WITH ROASTED PEPPER–FETA RELISH

Chef Dylan Giordan of Serafina and Cicchetti offers this recipe for lamb rubbed with the spice mixture ras el hanout, *which translates as "top of the shop," referring to the best that a spice merchant has to offer. The relish is a delectable mix of sweet roasted peppers, salty feta, and olives that could also serve as a bruschetta topping or a tapas-style salad. Chef Giordan recommends using any leftover ras el hanout to season chicken or to stir into pumpkin soup.*

Relish

½ cup minced red onion

2 tablespoons red wine vinegar

4 red bell peppers

1 cup dry-cured olives, halved and pitted

1 cup feta cheese (about 4 ounces), crumbled

1 tablespoon chopped fresh oregano

1 tablespoon chopped fresh mint

½ cup extra-virgin olive oil

Salt and freshly ground black pepper

Ras el Hanout

1 teaspoon cumin seeds

1 teaspoon coriander seeds

6 cardamom pods, seeds only (or ¼ teaspoon seeds)

½ teaspoon fennel seeds

½ teaspoon black peppercorns

2 teaspoons sweet paprika

1 teaspoon ground cinnamon

½ teaspoon ground allspice

1 teaspoon turmeric

1 teaspoon cayenne pepper

1 teaspoon fine sea salt

½ teaspoon sugar

Lamb

4 lamb racks (8 ribs each)

Kosher salt

Olive oil, for sautéing

To make the relish, mix the onion and vinegar in a small bowl and set aside to marinate for 30 minutes. Meanwhile, preheat the broiler. Place the red bell peppers on a baking sheet and broil them until blistered and beginning to blacken, about 5 minutes. Rotate them one-quarter turn and place them back under the heat. Continue turning and broiling until the skin of the peppers is blistered and beginning to blacken all over, about 3 minutes per side. Put the still-hot peppers into a paper bag and roll the top to seal. Allow them to steam for 10 minutes or until cool enough to handle, then peel and seed them and slice them into strips about ¼ inch wide. Put them in a bowl and add the olives, feta, oregano, mint, olive oil, and the marinated onions with the vinegar. Season to taste with salt and pepper and set aside.

To make the ras el hanout, put the cumin, coriander, cardamom, fennel, and peppercorns in a dry skillet over medium heat. Toast them lightly, agitating the skillet constantly, until they are aromatic, about 2 minutes. Be careful not to burn them. Use a spice grinder to grind them to a fine powder, then add the paprika, cinnamon, allspice, turmeric, cayenne pepper, sea salt, and sugar, and mix together. Store any leftover spice mixture in an airtight container.

Preheat the oven to 400 degrees F. Lightly salt each rack of lamb and then rub each one with about 2 teaspoons of the spice mixture. Heat several tablespoons of olive oil in a large ovenproof sauté pan over medium-high heat, and sear the racks evenly on both sides, about 5 minutes per side. If your sauté pan isn't large enough to hold all four racks, sear them individually and then transfer them to a baking sheet. Roast the lamb in the oven for about 15 minutes, or until the internal temperature in the thickest part of the rack reaches 140 degrees F. Remove the lamb from the oven, tent loosely with foil, and let rest for 10 minutes. Cut the racks between each bone, and serve with the relish.

MAKES 8 SERVINGS

CREOLE SPICE–RUBBED PORK CHOPS

At Jeremy Hardy's Coastal Kitchen, most of the menu changes every three months as the kitchen takes a virtual trip to another coastal spot around the world. But Chef Todd Torgerson's faithful customers won't let him take these succulent chops off the menu. He serves them with classic pork chop accompaniments: mashed potatoes and seasonal vegetables.

½ cup light brown sugar

¼ cup plus 2 tablespoons granulated garlic, or 3 tablespoons garlic powder

2 tablespoons salt

1 tablespoon paprika

1 tablespoon freshly ground black pepper

¼ teaspoon fennel seeds

½ cup Worcestershire sauce

2 tablespoons canola oil

1 tablespoon cider vinegar

6 pork chops (about 5 ounces each)

In a large bowl, combine the brown sugar, garlic, salt, paprika, pepper, and fennel seeds. In a small bowl, whisk together the Worcestershire sauce, oil, and vinegar. Then whisk the wet ingredients into the dry. Add the pork chops and turn to coat them completely with the marinade. Cover tightly with plastic wrap and refrigerate overnight. If you can, turn them every few hours.

The next day, preheat your grill to high. Take the chops from the refrigerator about 20 minutes before you cook them and let them start to come to room temperature. When you are ready to cook, lift each chop from the marinade and allow the excess to drip off. Then place the chops on the hot grill and close the lid for 1 minute. Open the lid and rotate each chop 45 degrees, then close the lid for about another minute, until the chops are well marked (the cooking time will depend on the thickness of the chops and the heat of your grill). Turn the chops over, close the lid, and cook them for 1 minute. Again, rotate them 45 degrees and continue cooking. The chops are done when their internal temperature reaches 145 degrees F. Transfer them to a plate and cover them loosely with foil. Let the chops rest for about 5 minutes to redistribute the juices before serving.

MAKES 6 SERVINGS

LOKI FISH CO.

A Proven Passion for Northwest Salmon

Pete Knutson sits in the tight galley of his fishing boat, the *Njord* (named for the Norse god associated with the sea and fishing), moored at Seattle's Fisherman's Terminal. It's pouring rain outside, but inside it's warm and he's offering tea and espresso. It feels a bit like central casting sent over a Norwegian fisherman. Pete is movie-star handsome, aging with craggy wrinkles in all the right places. His long, wavy golden hair is turning gray and he has it pulled back in a ponytail. His bright blue eyes sparkle, especially when his language turns colorful.

Pete's maternal great-grandfather was a shipwright who came to Ballard from Norway to start a shipyard at the turn of the last century. His family eventually moved north to Bellingham, and Pete grew up in Everett. If you were a teenager in Everett in the 1970s, you worked in either the lumber or the fishing industries. The Knutsons had a lot of neighbors who were commercial fishermen, so Pete asked one of them for a job. In those days, Pete explains, "It was a really good way for a young guy to make a substantial chunk of money in a short period of time, and then you had the rest of the year to do something else."

For Pete, that something else was going to college. His mother, in particular, was thrilled when he went off to Stanford University in 1970, but he didn't last long. In 1972 he was expelled for protesting weapons production and the Vietnam War. He spent the next few years completing his BA at The New School in Manhattan; traveling in Europe, North Africa, and Japan; and living in Berlin, all the while supporting himself by coming home to fish. "I always gravitated back. Fishing was sort of my anchor, and it still is. Every year it kinda resets my clock."

Although he seemed to have slipped into it, "I was attracted to fishing because a lot of the characters were real cantankerous but very honest," Pete explains. "You get cheats and scoundrels like in any other industry, but there was something fundamentally honest about what these guys were doing, which was producing food." He was also feeling alienated from mainstream America because of his protest of the Vietnam War, and he felt "morally handicapped to really survive at a corporate job." Although he was by then working on a bigger boat and selling fish to larger companies, "You felt like it was fundamentally a good thing that you were doing, and that the resource was pretty well-managed. I felt like it was one thing I could do without exploiting somebody. I felt solid about it, like it was a right livelihood."

In 1977 Pete went back to school at the University of Washington, and between fishing seasons he worked on his PhD in anthropology. In 1979 he married Hing and bought his first fishing boat, the *Loki* (named for a shape shifter in Norse mythology who sometimes appears as a salmon). By the time they had their first son, Jonah, the family was completely dependent on his fishing income.

Wild salmon fishing is managed tightly. During the season (which runs from April through July), the fishermen are given forty-eight to seventy-two hours at a time to fish, and they race out "to fish really hard," Pete explains. "Sometimes we'll be dressing 2,500 fish during that time. And so the guys are just working their asses off and then I'm picking the fish out of the net, running the net, putting the net, setting it, catching, figuring out where the fish are. And I'm getting three or four hours of sleep a day. And we get this huge sleep deficit and you get in to the dock where we unload our fish, and we bring our trucks down and rent a forklift and unload and grade them and sort them and layer them with ice in insulated totes, and we fork them onto the back of a truck, and we send the trucks on the Alaska ferry to Bellingham. And in Bellingham they clean the totes out, shoot ice back in, and shoot the trucks back up to us." And then, three months later, when it's all done, Pete says, "You're just f—ing toasted. You can't even function." And then the price of wild salmon collapsed due to the increase in availability of farmed salmon.

Pete had been direct marketing for a number of years by then. He'd joined a fisherman's co-op in Ketchikan, but it had gone bankrupt after a botulism incident with canned salmon in England that had decimated their market. So Pete had gone door-to-door in Seattle to sell his salmon, eventually finding Solly Amon at Pure Food, a longtime tenant at Pike Place Market, who agreed to buy his whole catch. Big fishing companies tried hard to chase him away by refusing to sell him ice and making it difficult for him to get his catch to Seattle, but Pete persisted. A refrigeration company designed a small system for his boat so that he wouldn't need ice, and he found more customers in the Bay Area. Then, just when he thought he had the business figured out, the market was flooded with farmed salmon, and the big distributors did everything they could to make

sure that any wild salmon sold was theirs, even if it wasn't as good as Pete's. On the *Loki* and the *Njord*, the catch is bled and gutted right away, then quickly chilled to below freezing. As a result, the fish remain firm, pink, and beautifully fresh.

But the quality of his fish didn't seem to matter to the commercial enterprises buying most of the salmon, so to augment his income, Pete applied for teaching jobs. He sent out loads of resumes and got two letters of interest: one from MIT and one from Seattle Central Community College. In the end he stuck close to home as an adjunct professor at Seattle Central Community College. He describes himself as a maritime anthropologist interested in existentialism. "I like the anthropologists with perspectives grounded in traditional cultures that were very humanistic and small-scale. And they used that standpoint to critique the impersonality of American culture."

Pete sighs. "And then I realize, man! I am going to be working my ass off the next twenty years of my life." He feels a huge responsibility to his students, and believes that he is a more effective teacher because, like many of his students, he balances two lives. In addition to teaching and fishing, he's long been an activist in the fishing industry, arguing for the protection of salmon habitat, sustainable fisheries, and other marine conservation issues. And he brings his real-life experiences to the classroom. "I like to get people thinking about their own lives, be self-reflective, take some of these insights from traditional cultures and look at our own—make our own culture sort of strange to ourselves.

"And the minute I turn my grades in, in June, boom! I'm gone with my crewmen and we are heading north." The funny thing is, Pete says,

"When I am out of school, the other teachers and administrators talk about me as the fisherman. But when I'm down here [at Fisherman's Terminal], these guys talk about me as the professor."

Before Pete began teaching, he fished a longer season and would be away four or five months at a time. "It was stressful," he remembers. Hing would be alone with their sons. "Their growing up time went very fast for me because I was gone so much. And then you come back, and you don't even know where the cornflakes are, and they've developed this whole family economy without you." Their family dynamics were made even more complicated because Hing's parents are Chinese. Pete describes his Norwegian family as independent, very, very frugal, and quiet. Hing's Chinese family, Pete says, tend to pool their resources and are loud. The integration of those two cultures in the Knutson household "has been very interesting."

Over the years, Pete's sons, Jonah and Dylan, have become partners in the family business. Jonah spent many years as Pete's deckhand, and in 2006 he inherited the *Loki*. Although Dylan made the trip to Alaska with Pete a number of times, he'd usually stay home and help Hing sell fish. "So he just kind of grooved into the distribution role down here. He's very good with people, and he loves the farmers markets. He hires people and deals with customers and organizes everything. He's become really, really good at the whole thing."

Because they fished together for so many years, Pete recognizes that he had a closer (though often contentious) relationship with Jonah than with Dylan. But a couple of years ago Pete took a sabbatical, and he and Dylan traveled to China, where they visited Hing's family and then hiked the Himalayas. These days, Dylan fishes for Keta (chum) salmon with Pete in the Puget Sound in the fall, and handles the business side of Loki.

Knowing firsthand that the life of a fisherman is difficult, dangerous, and not particularly lucrative, how does Pete feel about Jonah following so directly in his footsteps? "I understand it," Pete nods. "I think both of us really like the fact that we are independent and that we go out and do our thing. And we have control over our business. And the fish are beautiful. They come out of the water perfect. Our job is just to maintain that perfection all the way through. We are doing something that's meaningful and makes sense to us. And I think it makes sense to the people that buy our fish."

SOCKEYE SALMON WITH CHANTERELLES AND SUMMER PEPPERS

Maria Hines, James Beard Award–winning executive chef and owner of Tilth restaurant, has served salmon from Loki Fish Co. for years. She uses sockeye salmon here, but you can use any species of wild, sustainably caught salmon, such as king or coho. The fresh, bright flavors of sweet summer peppers balance the richness of the salmon in this stunning dish with its glorious shades of orange, yellow, and red.

6 large red bell peppers

4 sockeye salmon fillets (6 ounces each), skin on

Salt and white pepper

3 tablespoons unsalted butter

2 cups julienned (or very finely sliced) yellow onion (about 1 small)

4 cups julienned summer peppers (about 2 small bells), assorted colors

4 cups chanterelle or oyster mushrooms (about 8 ounces), cleaned, large ones torn

1 tablespoon minced garlic

¼ cup dry white wine

¼ cup chopped Italian parsley

Extra-virgin olive oil

4 lemon wedges

Preheat the broiler. Place the red bell peppers on a baking sheet and broil them until blistered and beginning to blacken. Rotate them one-quarter turn and place back under the heat. Continue turning and broiling until the skin of the peppers is blistered and beginning to blacken all over. Put the still-hot peppers into a paper bag and roll the top to seal. Allow them to steam for 10 minutes or until they're cool enough to handle, then peel and seed them.

Preheat the oven to 450 degrees F. Place the salmon fillets on a plate or baking sheet. Sprinkle both sides of the fillets with salt and white pepper. Set aside.

Using a food processor, purée the roasted red peppers. Add a drizzle of water if the peppers need help coming together. Pour the purée into a bowl, season it with salt and white pepper, and set it aside.

In a large sauté pan or skillet, heat the butter over medium heat. Add the onions and sauté until they soften and turn translucent, about 5 minutes. Add the julienned peppers and continue to sauté until the peppers start to soften, another 3 to 5 minutes. Add the mushrooms, garlic, and white wine. Stir to combine and continue cooking until the mushrooms have softened and their liquid has evaporated, about 5 minutes. Add salt and white pepper to taste. Add the chopped parsley and stir to combine. Remove the mixture from the heat, tent loosely with foil, and set aside in a warm place.

To cook the salmon, heat a large ovenproof skillet over high heat. Add 1 tablespoon olive oil and swirl to coat the pan. Carefully place the fillets in the pan, skin side down. (Do this in batches if your pan isn't big enough to hold all the fillets without crowding them.) Sear for 2 minutes, or until the skin crisps. Turn the fillets skin side up and put the pan in the oven; roast the salmon until it reaches the desired doneness, 3 to 5 minutes, depending on the thickness of the fillets.

To serve, spread a pool of the pepper purée in the center of each plate. Add a mound of the sautéed peppers and mushrooms. Place a salmon fillet, skin side up, on top of the mushroom mixture. Drizzle with olive oil and serve with a lemon wedge.

MAKES 4 SERVINGS

SWEET CORN, HEIRLOOM TOMATO, AND CHÈVRE SALAD WITH PAN-SEARED WILD SALMON

In this lovely summer dish from Chef Walter Pisano of Tulio restaurant, the sweetness of the corn and bright acidity of the tomatoes pair beautifully with the rich salmon and creamy chèvre. If you can't get big, meaty heirloom tomatoes, you can make this recipe with cherry tomatoes. Just halve them and toss them with the corn. Chef Pisano recommends pairing this with a pinot grigio or sauvignon blanc.

2 to 3 ears sweet corn, shucked

Pinch of sugar

3 tablespoons extra-virgin olive oil

1 tablespoon herbed wine vinegar or balsamic vinegar

Leaves from 2 sprigs fresh thyme

Sea salt and freshly ground black pepper

2 to 3 Brandywine heirloom tomatoes, sliced into ½-inch-thick "steaks" (enough for 2 to 3 slices per person)

½ cup crumbled chèvre (about 3 ounces)

2 tablespoons olive oil

4 wild salmon fillets (about 6 ounces each), skin removed

Fill a large pot with water and bring it to a boil over high heat. Add the corn and sugar, and when the water comes back to a boil, turn the heat down to medium and let the corn cook for 2 minutes. Remove the corn from the water, and when it is cool enough to handle, cut the kernels from the cobs. The easiest way to do this is to hold the cob upright in a deep, wide bowl. With a sharp knife, slowly make a downward cut close to the cob, slicing off several rows of kernels at a time. Continue around the cob. You should have about 2 cups of kernels.

Add the extra-virgin olive oil, vinegar, and thyme to the corn. Toss to combine and season to taste with salt and pepper. Arrange the tomato slices on 4 plates and season them with a pinch of salt. Spoon the corn mixture over the tomatoes and then sprinkle with the crumbled chèvre. Set the plates aside while you cook the salmon.

In a nonstick skillet, heat the olive oil over high heat. Season the salmon with salt and pepper. Place the fillets in the skillet presentation side down and immediately reduce the heat to medium. Let the fish begin to color on one side, 3 to 5 minutes, then reduce the heat to low, turn the fillets, and cook for about another 2 minutes, or until the fish reaches your desired doneness.

Arrange each fillet on a salad and serve right away.

MAKES 4 SERVINGS

TAYLOR SHELLFISH FARMS

Farming the Waterways

In the 1880s, Bill and Paul Taylor's great-grandfather began farming Olympia oysters in Puget Sound. Today the brothers run Taylor Shellfish Farms with their brother-in-law, Jeff Pearson. The largest producer of Manila clams in the world, they currently sell 8 million pounds a year. They have a state-of-the-art hatchery in Quilcene that produces mussel, oyster, and geoduck seed, another on the Big Island of Hawaii that grows clam seed, and farms all over Puget Sound, from Samish Bay in the north to Willapa Bay in the south. Recognized both for quality and consistency as well as for health and safety, their worldwide market is immense. But before "Oyster Bill" came along, the company relied entirely on wholesale distribution, so you'd be more likely to buy Taylor shellfish in Hong Kong than in Seattle.

Oyster Bill Whitbeck grew up in Connecticut, and although he'd visited Seattle once as a young boy to attend the World's Fair, he only moved here in 1977, the summer after he'd ridden his motorcycle across the country and seen Washington in its September splendor. In Connecticut he was a photographer with a studio in an old oyster house, but he was looking for a change. In Seattle he moved into the world of graphics and electronic prepress for a few years before returning to Connecticut to spend a year with his aging father. There he took a job with an oyster company, so when he returned to Seattle, he decided to stick with oysters.

The more he learned, the more fascinated he became.

In 2003 Oyster Bill approached Bill Taylor and told him he'd like to create a local market for Taylor's shellfish. These days, you'll see Taylor Shellfish at almost every Seattle food event, and they're members of the Seattle chapter of the Chef's Collaborative and of Slow Food. You can find their clams, oysters, mussels, and geoducks in restaurants throughout Western Washington, as well as in grocery stores and at their stores in Bow, Shelton, and in the Melrose Market in Seattle.

Bill makes the rounds for Taylor at Seattle's top restaurants. Instantly recognizable by his ruddy complexion, thick salt-and-pepper beard and mustache, and kindly Santa-like smile, if you see him anywhere else, he's probably shucking oysters.

On a perfect summer day, Bill introduced me to James Hall, one of the managers of Taylor's 2,000-acre Samish Bay farm. It was during one of the lowest tides of the year, and the mud flats seemed to stretch halfway to Lummi Island. Bald eagles floated along the tree line, the air smelled fresh, and the breezes off the bay brought just a sniff of brine. A tractor swept seaweed and algae so far off in the distance it appeared to move in slow motion without making a sound. A former firefighter, James is six foot two inches, and as he loped along the train track that runs across the back of Taylor's property, his enormous rubber boots folded below his knees, he took one step for every two of mine. When we stepped off the crushed rock embankment and down toward the water, I realized why we'd walked along the track and not through the farm. Although James's feet seemed to skim the surface, mine disappeared into the mud with a loud sucking sound. The trick is to walk quickly, lifting your feet before they can sink at all. James reassured me that the ground is not actually quicksand. Still, it takes a lot of energy and muscle to pull yourself out of the mud with each step, and the ground only gives you up reluctantly, with a big slurp.

James has been with Taylor for twenty-eight years. He's responsible for what grows on half the Samish Bay farm. First we walked through his clam beds, where plastic flex netting covers an area that's relatively firm and rocky. Using a short-tined pitchfork, James pried off a corner of the net and dug up a couple of inches of mud. In seconds he'd wiped clean a dozen clams in three sizes: market, submarket, and seed. James explained that clams take three years to mature, so each clam bed can hold three crops at a time. "It's like Social Security when you're digging through here. You take the big ones and leave the little ones, because you want to be able to come back and collect a paycheck."

Growing oysters is more complicated. All their seed comes from Taylor's hatchery (they call the FedEx guy "the stork"). Clam beds are seeded the way you seed a lawn, by broadcasting the seed and walking backward to avoid crushing them, and geoduck babies are placed in PVC tubes where they grow, protected from predators. Oyster seed, however, first goes into a tank of bay water that has been warmed to

72 degrees F. There it's mixed with oyster shells shucked the preceding year and then left outside to bleach dry. Over the course of about three days, the seed, which is so small it looks like ground black pepper, adheres to the large shell halves. Some shells will end up with just one or two seeds attached, others will hold dozens.

While Taylor grows Kumamotos, Olympias, and small amounts of European Flats and Virginicas, most of their oysters are Pacifics (*Crassostrea gigas*). They can grow them in different ways, occasionally resulting in oysters with different shapes and names. To grow most of the long, flat Pacifics, the seeded shells are piled on the deck of the *Ellen T.*, a flat-bottomed aluminum boat built in 1979 on Whidbey Island specifically for this farm. A high-powered hose with a fire nozzle sprays water pumped right from the bay onto the pile of oysters, sending them flying off the deck and into the water, where they sink to the bottom and grow. Two years later, the *Ellen T.* or the *Claire Ann*, an older wooden "oyster hoister," goes out at high tide with huge tubs that weigh 250 pounds empty, and sets them down where the oysters are maturing. At low tide, the tubs have settled; crews of watermen walk out to pick the oysters, piling them into baskets and filling the tubs. The boats return to pick up the tubs—which now weigh 1,250 pounds each—with their eagle claws, then bring them to the dock for cleaning and sorting. Once the oyster beds have been hand-picked, the oyster hoisters go back out to dredge the ground for any left behind. Then the ground is ready for seeding again.

Where the mud is too soft to grow oysters, an oyster long-line is used. Sections of braided rope three hundred feet long are pried open at close intervals and an oyster shell with at

least five babies attached is stuffed into each opening. As the rope twists closed, it locks the oyster shell in. The ropes are then stretched between stakes of PVC pipe in the soft mud where they'll stay until the babies are large enough to pick. "They bloom just like a flower," James explains. Some shells hold as many as thirty oysters, in which case some of them will fall to the ground as they crowd together on the mother shell. These fall-off oysters won't fatten like the ones on the rope, so after the hanging oysters are harvested, the crews return to pick up the fallen ones and take them to deep water to fatten for another four months.

In order to grow Pacifics into the deep-cupped oysters they call Shigoku, Taylor uses heavy mesh flip bags. Every twenty-four hours there are four tides (two high and two low). Bags filled with growing oysters are strung on ropes, and as the tide changes, the bags flip over and over. The oysters respond to all the movement by growing rounder instead of longer, resulting in deep cups. Whereas Kumamotos (the other small, deep-cupped oysters Taylor grows) take about three-and-a-half years to mature, Shigoku take only one.

Five months a year, in spring and summer, the lowest low tides (the best for working) are during daylight hours. In fall and winter, however, the best low tides are at night. The other two months of the year are the change-over tides, when half are in daylight and half are in the dark. In winter the crews wear lights on their hats. "Drive Chuckanut (the road that runs along the top of the bay) at low tide in the wintertime," James explains, "and it looks like a bunch of little white lights bouncing around. You've got the clam crew digging, the oyster guys picking, geoduck guys harvesting." In summer, when the weather is lovely and the work is in the daytime, crews harvest during low tide and pick up at high tide.

James thinks that's why neither of his children are in the business. "They saw a lot of Dad going to work, coming home, going to work, coming home." But James's brother, Eric Hall, also joined Taylor shortly after James did and today he runs the farm in Willapa; before that he ran the Dosewallips farm on the Hood Canal. There are many families like the Halls, with multiple family members and multiple generations employed by Taylor. There's also a large Latino community among Taylor's employees, as there is in many upland Washington farms.

All of Taylor's shellfish is grown sustainably, and the company's priorities include protecting the tidelands, keeping our waters and beaches clean, and educating the public on these issues. Taylor's farms and hatcheries are cutting edge, the company is constantly innovating (their newest mechanical clam digger runs on propane, uses vegetable oil, and is being built on Samish Island), and they share their knowledge with others in the industry all over the world. When Hurricane Katrina wiped out the oyster beds in the Gulf of Mexico, Taylor and other Pacific Northwest growers sent seed to the growers there. When Bill and James talk about Taylor, their pride in the company is palpable. They love the crowds who come to their annual Bivalve Bash, that growers come to the hatchery from all over the world to learn, that locals come to the farms to buy seed or something for dinner, and that they have so many loyal customers close to home. The company is family run—and these guys are family by choice.

MUSSELS WITH
ROASTED TOMATOES AND OREGANO

Chef Amy McCray serves these mussels at Eva Restaurant, which she owns with her husband, James Hondros. Roasting the tomatoes concentrates their sweetness, which in turn brings out the sweetness in the mussels. The steaming liquid is light and fresh, and lets the flavor of the mussels shine. Serve this dish with plenty of crusty bread, because you won't want to waste a drop of the precious shellfish broth. Try to cook the mussels the same day you buy them, but if you have to keep them overnight, store them in a bowl in the refrigerator, covered with a wet cloth. You'll want to serve two pounds of cooked mussels, so it's always a good idea to buy a few extra in case you have to discard any.

5 Roma tomatoes	1 tablespoon chopped fresh oregano
¾ cup olive oil	¾ cup white wine
2 pounds mussels	Salt
2 tablespoons chopped garlic	Crusty bread for serving

Preheat the oven to 400 degrees F. Cut the tops off the tomatoes, cut them in half lengthwise and scoop out the seeds. Place the tomatoes cut side down in a small roasting dish (an 8-inch-square baking dish works well) and pour the olive oil over them. Roast them for 20 to 25 minutes, until the skins blister and the tomato flesh is tender. If the oil splatters too much, you can cover the dish loosely with foil. Let the tomatoes cool in the oil, then remove them with a slotted spoon, reserving the oil. Pull the skins off the tomatoes and discard. Chop the tomatoes into ½-inch pieces and set aside.

Before cleaning the mussels, check for dead ones by tapping on any that are open; they should close immediately. Discard any that don't as well as any that are broken. To clean the mussels, fill a bowl with cold water and salt it well. Add the mussels and swirl them around for 1 minute. Let them sit in the water in the refrigerator for 30 minutes to expel any sand or grit. Rinse them well in cold water, scrub the shells to remove any dirt and barnacles, and remove the beards by pulling them toward the hinge. Set aside.

Heat ¼ cup of the reserved roasted tomato oil in a large, deep sauté pan (with a lid) over medium heat. Add the garlic and sauté until softened, about 1 minute. Add the mussels, tomatoes, and oregano and toss them together. Add the wine, turn the heat up to high, and cover the pan. Steam until the mussels open, 3 to 5 minutes. Check to make sure all the mussels have opened and discard any that remain closed. Taste the liquid and add salt to taste. Serve the mussels in shallow bowls with a generous amount of the steaming liquid poured over them.

MAKES 2 MAIN COURSE SERVINGS OR 4 SERVINGS AS AN APPETIZER

BLACKENED OYSTERS WITH CHIPOTLE AÏOLI AND PICO DE GALLO

Jeremy McLachlan, chef at Salty's, recommends pairing this fresh, spicy appetizer with a cooling Porter-style beer. The recipe makes plenty of aïoli, which Chef McLachlan suggests using for dipping fries or topping burgers and tacos. You may have some extra "pico," too—so to turn the dish into a main course, just sauté more oysters and serve them over creamy grits.

Chipotle Aïoli

½ cup mayonnaise

1 egg yolk

1 clove garlic, minced

1 chipotle pepper in adobo sauce (from a can)

1 teaspoon coriander seeds, toasted

¼ cup canola oil

¼ cup chopped cilantro

1 lime, zested and juiced (about 1 teaspoon zest and 1½ tablespoons juice)

Salt

Pico De Gallo

2 Roma tomatoes, seeded and cut into ¼-inch dice

½ small sweet onion, cut into ¼-inch dice (about ½ cup)

¼ cup chopped cilantro

½ jalapeño pepper, finely diced

Juice of 1 lime (about 1½ tablespoons)

Salt

Blackened Oysters

1 tablespoon canola oil

16 medium oysters, shucked

2 to 3 tablespoons Cajun-style dry spice mix, preferably Salty's Blackening Spice

To make the aïoli, put the mayonnaise, egg yolk, and garlic in the bowl of a food processor and blend for 3 minutes. Add the chipotle and coriander seeds and blend for 1 minute. With the food processor still running, slowly drizzle in the oil, then add the cilantro, lime zest and juice, and salt to taste. Set aside.

To make the pico de gallo, gently combine the tomatoes, onion, cilantro, jalapeño, and lime juice. Season with salt to taste. (Remove the jalapeño seeds to make a mild salsa; leave them in to make it spicy.)

Heat the canola oil in a large sauté pan over medium-high heat. Pat the oysters dry on paper towels, dust them with the powdered spice mix, and carefully place them in the hot pan. Sear for 1 to 2 minutes per side, until the oysters plump up and get a bit of color. Arrange 4 oysters on each of 4 appetizer plates, top each with a dollop of aïoli and a bit of pico de gallo, and serve right away.

MAKES 4 SERVINGS AS AN APPETIZER

FRUIT

Here in Washington we are incredibly fortunate to be able to eat fresh, local fruit all year long. In earliest summer we start with strawberries and work our way through more varieties of juicy, sweet raspberries, blackberries, blueberries (and yet more strawberries) than people living elsewhere know exist. Approaching mid-summer, stone fruits grow in abundance all throughout the central part of our state: peaches and nectarines so ripe the juice runs like water; apricots and cherries so sweet they taste like jam or candy; plums and pluots that snap when you bite into them, the tender flesh bursting through their taut skins. These are the kinds of fruits that show their true merits only when they are tree-ripened, hand-picked, and handled with tender loving care each step of the way, from field to farmers market, until the moment you bite into them.

As summer deepens, the dry heat east of the Cascade Mountains is perfect for producing sweet, juicy melons, and every year it seems there are more and more varieties available. The perfume that wafts from a tub of sun-warmed melons is one of the most intoxicating, welcome signs of summer. Fruits like these bruise and deteriorate easily, so time and travel are their worst enemies.

Then apple and pear season hits, and the whole world knows it. According to the Washington Apple Commission, we harvest about 4 billion pounds of apples a year! Although most are Red Delicious, there are countless heirloom varieties available from smaller growers. More than half the pears grown in the United States are grown in Washington. Most are Bartlett and d'Anjou, but again, there are many other varieties available as well. Pears ripen off the tree and apples store beautifully, so it's easy to enjoy these fruits all winter long and into spring. And then—lucky us—the cycle begins again.

ALM HILL GARDENS

Growing a Farm

It's unusually warm this April morning. Gretchen Hoyt stands in a field of multicolored tulips and squints into the sun, her long, silvery gray hair neatly pulled back and bundled. She turns to speak as the breeze catches the wisps of hair framing her face, and her light blue eyes open to reveal a shade that matches the sky. With a hand outstretched, she recites the list of tulips in bloom like poetry as she points them out: "Judith Leister, Elegant Lady, Dulles Minuet, Temple of Beauty."

Gretchen looks at home in the field because she is. Thirty-five years ago she started Alm Hill Gardens with her husband, Ben Craft. She'd moved home to Washington from California where she'd been raising a young family and running one of the very first self-service gas stations. There she'd had a little garden, "And I just planted a seed and put a little water in it and here was all this response, and I felt so excited! It was so moving, and I felt so fed by the work that it made me think that this is what I want to do."

First she rented twenty acres of pasture in Olympia that turned out to be salty. Then she moved to five acres where she lived with a group of college students and grew a large garden, but it still didn't feel right. Her brother was attending Western Washington University, and she went up with a friend to visit him. Her friend also had friends up in Everson, where they introduced her to Ben, who had come over one day for water because he had none at the geodesic dome house he was building for himself. Gretchen says she was immediately drawn to him.

Soon after, Gretchen moved in with Ben at his house on sixty-two acres he owned with his father. For years they'd leased it to run cattle, and Ben used to come up to walk the land. He loved it and wanted to live on it, so with his father as his partner, and money earned from a paper route he'd had since he was ten, they bought the property before he left for Vietnam.

When he met Gretchen, Ben was head mechanic and supervisor on the night shift at a cannery. They canned beans, carrots, and beets, Gretchen explains, "which to this day he can hardly bear to eat." Someone he worked with told him you could make $20,000 on an acre of raspberries, and since Gretchen didn't care what they were growing as long as they were growing something, it sounded too good to pass up. They planted an acre of raspberries, but that first year the neighbor's cattle ate all their plants practically down to the ground. They didn't make a penny.

The next year they realized that there was a difference of only four cents a pound between what they'd pay their pickers and what they'd earn from the cannery, so they took out the back seat of their Studebaker, filled it with flats of berries, and took them to Pike Place Market. Still, they earned a tiny fraction of what they'd expected, with only a month of raspberry income. Although their goal was to farm full time, Ben continued at the cannery and Gretchen held all sorts of jobs, including delivering a paper route and driving a school bus. Over time, Gretchen says, they just gradually added crops on either end of the raspberry season, until they could go year-round.

Gretchen and Ben raised four kids on the farm: Joshua, who runs his own farm called Nooksack Nine; Katie, a nursing student who works at the Alm Hill Gardens' stall at farmers markets on the weekends; and Gretchen's sons from her first marriage, Patrick and Greg. "If you were going to eat here, you were going to work here," Gretchen says, and until the mid-'90s their children and other local kids did all the picking. But of the four of them, only Joshua has chosen farming as a career, and he came to that realization after many years working construction. He farms ten acres, but has no interest in taking over the complex systems of year-round farming at Alm Hill.

When Gretchen and Ben realized that none of their children were going to stay on at their farm, they needed to figure out a transition plan. They had been farming for thirty years and were ready to slow down. In fact, Ben was thinking about quitting farming completely, wanting to reclaim his summers, tired of dealing with the risk of bad weather. He began growing hothouse tomatoes, which renewed his interest somewhat, because at least he was protected from the elements. The tomatoes quickly paid for their greenhouses.

Around 1995 they began growing tulips, and shortly afterward they met a Dutchman in Sumner who offered to teach them the intricacies necessary to force bulbs (to bring them to flower out of season). Since they already had the greenhouses, forcing flowers seemed like an obvious next step. "So we started doing that and I can tell you a lot of different ways to fail, because we have," Gretchen laughs. Every year they learned something new, slowly mastering

the process. They started with irises, then tulips, and they now grow 350,000 tulips each year. That sounds like a lot, and it certainly keeps them busy, but it actually makes them one of the smallest tulip growers in the state.

For the next step in their transition plan, Gretchen and Ben contacted Washington FarmLink (a program that connects aspiring farmers and landowners and helps build sustainable farms) hoping to find someone interested in working with them, learning how to farm, and then eventually taking over. But no one seemed to want more than a summer experience, until they met Clayton Burrows. Clayton is the executive director of Growing Washington, a nonprofit community organization that focuses on sustainable agriculture, environmental and cultural preservation, and helping other like-minded nonprofits organize, plan, build, and grow. Clayton first came on as an apprentice; in 2007 he began leasing most of Alm Hill's land and its growing operations.

Since they were not yet ready to retire, Gretchen and Ben held on to the floral side of the farm. In 2009 they greatly improved the efficiency of their flower-forcing operations by building a large cooler and cutting shed right next to the greenhouses. Not only did their business improve, but it has made their lives much easier, and so much less physically demanding that they see themselves continuing in the flower business for at least another ten years. Today they force tulips, hyacinths, peonies, Asian lilies, and calla lilies. As Gretchen and Ben expanded their repertoire over the years from berries to all kinds of produce, they embraced the challenges of learning how to grow and harvest each variety well.

Now they feel lucky to rise to the challenges again as they learn about different varieties

of flowers. Gretchen also grows sunflower sprouts (for eating) in the greenhouses, and lilacs and a variety of annuals outside. The couple works mostly from December through June, then get a little time to themselves. Jay Dennison, Growing Washington's president, and Clayton run the majority of the farm with the help of a team of Latino farmers who have worked with Ben and Gretchen for years.

When Gretchen finally found herself with a little bit of time on her hands, she seized the opportunity to pursue projects that had always interested her. Among these was a food bank farm. For years, a gleaning group called Small Potatoes (now a program of the Bellingham Food Bank) had come through Alm Hill Gardens and picked beans, berries, and other produce for local social agencies. Gretchen joined forces with their founder to farm three acres offered to them by Cascade Christian Services. They planted the field and organized a team of volunteers, and Growing Washington has since partnered with the Bellingham Food Bank to run the food bank farm.

Gretchen also started a Farm to School program that Growing Washington has embraced, in which kids get fresh, local food in their schools, and the grant money from the USDA that pays for it finds its way directly to local farmers. Since 2009, Alm Hill has sold to the Auburn School District, which serves 23,000 students, and to Western Washington University.

As she walks along the rows of blooming tulips, clumps of soil crunching under her feet, Gretchen carries an enormous bunch of tulips under one arm, using the other hand to pick by snapping the stems all the way at the ground. It's back-breaking work, even if she does make it look easy. "Flowers aren't heavy, and people are happy when they are buying flowers," Gretchen smiles, "so it's working out well for us."

BIBB LETTUCE SALAD WITH ORANGE-HAZELNUT VINAIGRETTE

When you have a truly fine green salad in a restaurant, it's a sign that the restaurateur and his staff are attuned to providing excellence throughout their menu. Executive Chef James Drohman serves this crowd-pleaser at both Le Pichet and Café Presse, and he knows that because the salad is so simple, the quality of the ingredients is paramount. Drohman uses Duchilly hazelnuts from Holmquist Hazelnut Orchards, and he gets his Bibb lettuce from Frank's Quality Produce, which buys from various organic growers. The salad should be very lightly dressed, so there will be plenty of leftover vinaigrette. Just store it in the refrigerator and use often.

1 large head very fresh Bibb lettuce (also called butter lettuce)

Scant 1 cup hazelnuts

1 cup orange juice

1 small shallot, roughly chopped

½ cup sherry vinegar

1 tablespoon Dijon mustard

1½ teaspoons kosher salt

¼ teaspoon freshly ground black pepper

About ½ cup soy oil

To prepare the lettuce, remove any dead or damaged leaves, but leave the head intact. Wash it carefully, making sure to check the interior leaves near the base for dirt. Let the lettuce drain upside down on paper towels or in a colander in the refrigerator for about 1 hour. As the lettuce chills, it will become wonderfully crisp.

Preheat the oven to 350 degrees F. Toast the hazelnuts on a baking sheet until they begin to color and smell nutty, about 12 minutes. Set them aside to cool, then roughly chop them. Divide the chopped nuts into two portions: a little less than half will go into the dressing and the remaining nuts will be sprinkled on the salads at serving time. While the nuts are toasting, bring the orange juice to a boil in a small saucepan over medium heat and simmer until reduced by half, then set it aside to cool completely.

To make the vinaigrette, put the reduced orange juice, the smaller amount of hazelnuts, shallot, vinegar, mustard, salt, and pepper in a blender. Blend at high speed until creamy and smooth. With the blender running, slowly drizzle in the oil until the vinaigrette has the consistency of heavy cream. The amount of oil required may be slightly more or less. If it gets too thick, you can add a little water to thin it. (Be careful not to let the blender run too long, as the vinaigrette will break if it gets too warm.) Taste and add more salt or pepper if needed.

When ready to serve, cut the core from the bottom end of the lettuce. Separate the leaves and tear them into smaller pieces. Make sure that there is no water on the leaves. Toss the lettuce with a little vinaigrette and salt and pepper to taste. Arrange the lettuce on individual salad plates or on a large serving dish. Sprinkle the remaining chopped hazelnuts over the top and serve right away.

MAKES 4 TO 6 SALAD SERVINGS AND 1½ CUPS VINAIGRETTE

BLUEBERRY PANNA COTTA WITH RASPBERRY GELÉE

Chef Robin Leventhal served this striking layered dessert at "An Incredible Feast 2010," a remarkable food event that benefits the Neighborhood Farmers Market Alliance and the Good Farmer Fund. She was paired with Hayden Farms, which provided the plump fragrant berries she used in this ethereal, barely sweet dessert. While competing on the Bravo TV show Top Chef, *Robin was told by Nigella Lawson that "a perfect panna cotta should jiggle like the inside of a woman's thigh." Robin used that advice to perfect this star anise–scented custard with its bright, herbaceous raspberry gelée.*

3 cups whole milk, divided

¼ cup plus 1 tablespoon sugar

1 cinnamon stick

1 wide strip lemon peel (do not include white pith)

1 cardamom pod, pinched to expose seeds

1 star anise pod

1¾ teaspoons powdered gelatin

½ cup cold heavy whipping cream

1½ cups blueberries, plus extra for garnish

Gelée

1 cup water

¼ cup sugar

1½ teaspoons chopped fresh rosemary

1 cup raspberries

2 tablespoons cold water

1 teaspoon powdered gelatin

Heat 2¾ cups of the milk in a saucepan over medium heat just until there are bubbles forming around the edge of the pan. Remove from the heat and add the sugar, cinnamon, lemon peel, cardamom pod, and star anise. Stir to dissolve the sugar. Cover and let steep 30 minutes. About 10 minutes before the end of the steeping time, put the remaining ¼ cup cold milk into a small bowl and sprinkle the gelatin over it.

After the 30 minutes are up, remove the cover from the saucepan and gently reheat the milk until bubbles form around the edge of the pan. Remove the pan from the heat, add the gelatin mixture, and stir, making sure the gelatin completely dissolves. Strain the milk to remove the aromatics and then add the cold cream. Stir gently to mix (whisking or stirring vigorously will make the milk mixture foamy, which you want to avoid).

Select 8 clear glass, wide-mouth dishes (glass ramekins, parfait glasses, or martini glasses work well) and set them on a tray. They should hold 6 to 8 ounces of liquid (1 cup or slightly less) each. Divide the blueberries between them, then pour the panna cotta mixture over the berries. Refrigerate the glasses for at least 3 hours, or preferably overnight.

Make the gelée after the panna cottas have set up completely. Bring the 1 cup of water, the sugar, and rosemary to a boil in a small saucepan. Remove from the heat, add the raspberries, and let steep for 15 minutes. Meanwhile, sprinkle the gelatin over the 2 tablespoons of cold water and leave it to soften for at least 5 minutes. Add the softened gelatin to the saucepan and gently reheat the mixture just until the gelatin melts (do not let the mixture simmer or boil, or the gelatin will not set). Pour the mixture into a blender and purée well (be careful because warm liquids rise in the blender quickly). Strain the purée through the finest strainer you have into a small, clear plastic or glass container. Let the purée sit for 10 minutes, undisturbed, then carefully skim off the pale foam that rises to the top. You won't be able to get it all, but the dessert will be more beautiful if you just use the intensely colored part. Top each panna cotta with the raspberry gelée and chill in the refrigerator to set, at least 2 hours.

Garnish the top of each glass with a few fresh blueberries.

MAKES 8 SERVINGS

BALSAMIC STRAWBERRIES

While Dana Cree was pastry chef at Poppy Restaurant in Seattle, she made these marinated fresh strawberries at the height of summer, when local strawberries with names like Hoods, Sumas, Shuksan, and Fire Cracker flood the stores and farmers markets. She warns that because these varieties tend to be delicate and perishable; they should be eaten the same day they are prepared. But that shouldn't be a problem: these peppery, sweet strawberries are delicious on breakfast oatmeal, with Greek yogurt or cheesecake, or with a simple scoop of vanilla ice cream.

1 pint fresh local strawberries (Shuksan are Cree's favorite variety)

1 to 2 tablespoons high-quality, syrupy aged balsamic vinegar

2 tablespoons sugar

A few grinds of black pepper

Quickly rinse the strawberries in a bowl of cool water to wash off any dirt. Let them dry on a towel.

Cut the green tops from the strawberries and slice each berry lengthwise in half. Place them in a bowl and gently toss with the vinegar, sugar, and black pepper. (If your balsamic is thick and sweet, use the full 2 tablespoons. If it is thin and quite acidic, use a little less.) Set aside for at least 30 minutes to allow the flavors to mingle and the strawberries to macerate in the balsamic syrup.

MAKES 1¾ CUPS STRAWBERRIES

PIPITONE FARMS

An Evangelical Organic

Every Tuesday at lunchtime, the Wenatchee Chapter of Order Sons of Italy in America plays bocce ball and drinks wine in the shade of young apricot trees on Pipitone Farms in Rock Island, just outside Wenatchee. Most of the Sons are retired, but their host is not. In fact, the hours that Jerry Pipitone spends preparing for the meeting, playing the game, and napping afterward are the only time he takes off each week.

Jerry is no stranger to hard work. He describes himself, with a self-deprecating chuckle, as a malcontent and a Jack-of-all-trades. He has fourteen years sea time as a tugboat sailor and served in the military. He's a journeyman outside machinist. "If you need your crane repaired, if you need some torpedo tubes mounted on your Coast Guard cutter, I'm the guy." He even sold tires for a while, but hated every minute of it. "Now my oath is I will only sell what I produce."

In 1948, when Jerry was eight years old, his family moved to Seattle from southern Wisconsin. Jerry's father's older brother had come out with the Army in about 1920 and had fallen in love with salmon fishing. It took him almost twenty years to finally move west, but when he did, his little brother soon followed. "And shortly thereafter," Jerry reports with mock seriousness, just barely erasing his dimples, "it was determined that the entire city of Seattle was not big enough for these two Sicilian brothers." Eventually his parents divorced and his father moved back to Wisconsin, but Jerry and his mother stayed.

Jerry calls himself a product of the back-to-the-land movement of the 1970s. He grew up in West Seattle, and still considers himself an Alki Point boy, but moved to the Wenatchee area in 1974, partly as a reaction to the fatal lifestyle choices some of his friends were making in the big city. He found a job picking apples in Monitor, but that turned out to be a rocky introduction to farming (he was fired for bruising the notoriously tender Golden Delicious), and he eventually got a job doing metal work in a manufacturing company and started gardening on the side. "One day, I had two hundred pounds of garlic hanging in my garage, and I went, 'I'm a farmer!'" For a long time it was just part-time, but constantly expanding, until he married his current wife, Andrea, in 1985; they bought five acres of old apricot trees in Rock Island in 1987.

Jerry loves the location—his fruit is ready for picking a week earlier than anywhere else in the state, and the view from his back door is of the twenty-mile-long low mountain range called Badger Mountain, which an artist friend of his painted for the farm's label.

These days he grows vegetables in rows between the fruit trees. He sells garlic and shallots (the real, old-fashioned, bulb-grown Dutch Red variety), but the rest of his vegetables are for his processing. Jerry and Andrea built a commercial kitchen on their farm, where they produce an organic line of low-sugar jams called Yum, fruit syrups, and chutneys. They also dry their fruit and tomatoes and sell them year-round.

Even before you can see the top of Rock Island Red's table at the Ballard and University District farmers markets, you can tell when the peaches and apricots are ripe. Andrea makes shirts for Jerry that are the fruit equivalents of flowered Hawaiian ones. All summer long, he's his own best advertisement for what is fresh off the trees.

It may not be acceptable to choose from among your children, but Jerry has no problem talking about his favorite varieties of fruit. Among the apricots, he loves the Rilands, originally developed in 1920 in Rock Island (the name is a contraction). Since then, they've been planted everywhere, Jerry explains, but primarily as the great pollinator. It's rare to find the actual fruit for sale because it doesn't ship well. Rilands have nothing going for them except truly excellent flavor, Jerry offers with a rueful laugh, "which is not a market characteristic." He also grows Rivals, Tiltons, Tomcots, and an experimental variety that he's affectionately named BR549, after a country music band, because he can't remember what it's really called. He's happy to report he cut down the last of the old Perfections, a variety he describes as having all those perfect market characteristics, but no flavor.

Jerry's original block of Rilands was planted in 1946. As the trees age, they become more expensive to maintain—productivity declines while they grow immense amounts of new wood that requires a lot of pruning (an apricot tree pruned correctly is basically a new tree every five years). So he's planted younger blocks that are starting to produce (and shade the aforementioned bocce court), and he's begun removing some of the older trees.

Pipitone Farms has somewhere between eight hundred and one thousand fruit trees, two-thirds of which are apricots. Jerry also grows prune plums, but he doesn't sell them fresh anymore because he can't keep up with the demand for dried. He grows nectarines and a variety of peaches, including the popular Red Haven and Elberta (the classic canning peach), but his favorite is the Rio Oso Gem, which "has this real rich nectarine deep flavor and beautiful color. The red streaks from the dark red skin run right through the flesh sometimes and down to the pit. It's gorgeous."

In the early 1970s, before leaving Seattle, Jerry read Rachel Carson's *Silent Spring* and was both horrified and inspired. Originally published in 1962, it is often pointed to as the impetus behind the contemporary environmental movement. It made an enormous impression on him; as a result he has always used and promoted entirely organic practices in gardening and farming. He adheres to the basic organic principle put forth by J. Rodale that healthy plants, grown on healthy soil, are naturally resistant to disease and insect infestation. He improves the soil by bringing in dump trucks of horse manure, using compost created from the waste from his commercial kitchen operation, and growing cover crops. One of the keys to the National Organic Program (which certifies organic farms) is to prove that he is improving his soil, not mining it. He's also learned that the insects take care of themselves. "Every spring it's the same thing. It's, oh my God, look at the aphids. Leaf ends all curled up. And I just grit my teeth and I turn around and walk away. And I come back three, four days later, and they're all dead. There's a jillion insects that are predatory, and the unbalance comes from general use pesticides."

But in the years that he's been farming, Jerry has seen a great deal of change, and he believes there's a lot of economic opportunity for Washington in this arena. He speculates that the largest fruit grower in the state will probably go completely organic within the next couple of years. While he's a proponent of organics for the environmental impact, he notes that when the big producers go organic, they'd have the power to bring the whole state over—that would be a marketing coup. Imagine, he says, if a sticker on a piece of fruit that says "Washington" meant it was organic.

Although he's committed to farming, evangelizing organic practices, and ensuring the survival and success of farmers markets (he helped found the Wenatchee farmers market and serves on the board of Seattle's Neighborhood Farmers Market Alliance), Jerry doesn't know what will happen to his own farm when he's ready to retire. He has two children from his first marriage, helped raise (and has remained close to) his second wife's four children, and Andrea has three children from her previous marriage, but not one of them has any interest in farming.

Jerry laughingly describes farming as a disease, and says there's no logical reason why he does it. Just about every job he's ever had paid better. However, he says, "I like to point out that my boss now is a really good guy." And growing things is a huge reward that he doesn't think he'll ever get used to. "I'll tell you," he says, "the joy of seeing the baby plants coming up every year is difficult to describe. I love what I do absolutely. I get up with enthusiasm every day." Although selling at the farmers markets is a remarkable amount of work, he's realized that not only would he not make any money at all if he sold wholesale, but he loves dealing with his customers directly. "I get ego strokes that count. And I never got that on a tugboat." He enjoys nothing more than hearing, "Those are the absolute best apricots I've ever had in my life!"

SPICED ALBACORE TUNA WITH STONE FRUIT CHUTNEY

Here in the Pacific Northwest, albacore tuna and stone fruits are both at their peak in the middle of the summer. Chef Jeffrey Wilson at Table 219 prepares this sweet and sour jewel-toned India-inspired dish with fruit he gets from Pence Orchards. Because troll-caught Pacific albacore tuna is not only high in omega-3 fatty acids, but is also sustainable, we can feel even better about eating this mild, buttery fish.

1 cup jasmine rice

Olive oil, for sautéing

2 bunches scallions, trimmed and chopped, white and green parts separated

4 cloves garlic, minced

3 to 3½ pounds assorted peaches, apricots, and plums, pitted and chopped into ¾- to 1-inch pieces (about 7 cups)

Kosher salt and freshly ground black pepper

6 teaspoons Chinese black vinegar (or substitute high-quality, syrupy aged balsamic vinegar)

1 albacore tuna loin (about 1½ pounds), or 6 tuna steaks (about 1 inch thick)

1 tablespoon garam masala (a little less if using steaks)

Rinse the rice in a sieve until the water runs clear, then drain it well and cook according to the instructions on the package. Set the rice aside, covered, to stay warm.

While the rice is cooking, make the chutney. Add about 2 tablespoons olive oil to a large sauté pan over medium-low heat. Add the white part of the scallions and the garlic and cook slowly until soft but not colored, about 10 minutes. Add the fruit and continue to cook, stirring occasionally, just until the fruit softens and begins to fall apart, about 15 minutes. Remove from the heat, stir in the green parts of the scallions, and season lightly with salt and pepper. Cover to keep warm.

Season the tuna with salt, dust it with the garam masala and pat to adhere. In a large sauté or frying pan over high heat, add just enough olive oil to thinly coat the bottom of the pan; heat until smoking. Carefully add the tuna (cut the loin crosswise in half if it won't fit in one piece) and sear each side quickly to keep it as rare as possible, no more than 1 minute per side. Turn off the heat and remove the tuna from the pan.

To serve, cut the tuna into ½-inch slices. Spoon some of the rice into the middle of each plate and surround it with the chutney. Top the rice with slices of tuna and drizzle the vinegar over the dish.

MAKES 6 SERVINGS

APRICOT SORBET

Adria Shimada makes this creamy, refreshing sorbet with Jerry Pipitone's apricots. It's one of the most popular flavors at her mobile ice creamery, Parfait. Be sure to use the very ripest fruit you can find. Adria sources as many of her ingredients locally as she can: in addition to the stone fruits from Jerry Pipitone, Adria gets spearmint from Full Circle Farm in Carnation; raspberries, strawberries, and blueberries from Alm Hill Gardens in Everson; and honey from Ballard Bee Company in Seattle.

2 pounds ripe fresh apricots

1 cup water

1 cup plus 2 tablespoons sugar

Freshly squeezed juice from ½ lemon (about 2 tablespoons)

Wash the apricots thoroughly. Remove the pits and then quarter the fruit. In a heavy-bottomed pot, add the water to the apricots and cook, uncovered, over medium heat until very soft, 10 to 12 minutes, stirring occasionally. Remove from the heat and add the sugar and lemon juice; stir to completely dissolve the sugar. Let the mixture cool to room temperature, then purée it using either an immersion blender, a food processor, or a blender. Chill thoroughly in the refrigerator (at least 4 hours or overnight).

Freeze in an ice cream maker according to the manufacturer's instructions.

MAKES ABOUT 1 QUART SORBET

ROASTED CHERRY AND GRAPPA ICE CREAM

Ethan Stowell, chef and owner of Staple & Fancy, Tavolàta, How to Cook a Wolf, and Anchovies & Olives, gets his Bing cherries from Frank's Produce in the Pike Place Market. Roasting the cherries intensifies their flavor, and the dairy products mellow the bite of the grappa, letting its flavors shine. The resulting ice cream is deliciously intense, very creamy, and pale lavender in color.

1 pound fresh Bing cherries, washed and dried

1 tablespoon olive oil

2 cups heavy cream

2 cups whole milk

1 cup sugar

½ vanilla bean, split lengthwise and seeds scraped

1 teaspoon salt

8 large egg yolks, at room temperature

¼ cup grappa

Preheat the oven to 400 degrees F. Toss the cherries in a bowl with the olive oil, then spread them out on a baking sheet. Roast the fruit until the cherries begin to wrinkle and ooze their juices, 20 to 25 minutes. Pour the fruit and juices into a bowl to cool. When the cherries are cool enough to handle, remove the stems and pits and roughly chop the fruit. Refrigerate until cold.

In a large saucepan, combine the cream, milk, sugar, vanilla bean and seeds, and salt; bring to a boil over medium heat. Meanwhile, whisk the egg yolks in a large bowl. Keep a careful eye on the milk mixture as it nears the boil, because it will froth up quickly. When the cream mixture has reached a full boil, remove it from the heat and ladle about 1 cup of the hot cream into the bowl with the yolks, whisking constantly. Then pour the yolk mixture back into the pot with the cream, whisking constantly until well blended. Cook the mixture over medium-low heat, stirring gently and constantly with a wooden spoon or spatula, until the foam subsides and the mixture thickens slightly and coats the back of the spoon. Strain the mixture into a clean container, using a fine-mesh sieve to remove any bits of cooked egg and the vanilla bean. Add the grappa and the cherries and their juices; stir to combine. Refrigerate this mixture until it is completely cold, then freeze it in an ice cream maker according to the manufacturer's instructions.

MAKES ABOUT 1½ QUARTS ICE CREAM

BOOTH CANYON ORCHARD

Sweet Serendipity

Back in 1995, before Booth Canyon Orchard, there was just a picture-perfect little white farmhouse for sale near Twisp with an acre and a half of pear trees in the backyard. And there was Stina Booth, who, after years of working seasonally all over the place, doing all sorts of things, got tired of living in bunkhouses and out of her car, and went house-hunting. When her father discovered that the little house sat at the end of a canyon called Booth, Stina Booth knew it was meant to be.

Happy to be putting down roots, she continued working for the Forest Service but embraced the orchard in her backyard. "I'll pick them, prune them, and make money, how hard can that be?" she thought. "It involves a little more than that," she laughs now.

So Stina read books, asked her extension agent for advice, and peppered an organic supply house in Wenatchee with questions. She met another orchardist up the Twisp River and they talked a bit, too. "It's a pretty slow learning curve on tree fruit because you only have the growing season; you pretty much only have one opportunity to do each particular task. You may not see the results of that for another year, and then you can't try something different until the following year. It's not like you messed up the lettuce, so you till it under, and you try it again. You've only got one shot at it this year."

In 2000, Stina married John Richardson and they bought five acres of apple orchard next door. By this time she'd increased the pear orchard to three acres, had the farm certified organic, and was selling at the University District farmers market. But she still had a lot to learn, so she left the Forest Service and spent the next two years commuting to the tree-fruit program at Wenatchee Valley College. Although the program is geared toward large-scale industrial apple farms, the basic rules of horticulture still apply.

Just as Stina was learning about the Washington apple industry, it was going through a huge dip. "No one was making anything on Reds and Goldens. They were barely making anything on Galas and Braeburns. So I knew we had to go in this niche market direction." She pored over fruit catalogs, which she calls fruit porn, noticing that most apple farmers were chasing the new red, sweet, and crunchy Honeycrisp type of apple—but decided to go the other way, toward tart heirloom apples instead. "We tried to have early and late, sweet and tart, reds and yellows, some russets. We tried to hit a spectrum of varieties, and our goal was the stuff that tasted the best. So we grafted a bunch, and they started coming into production, and some didn't make it, and some weren't good enough, some didn't taste great, and in some cases they just didn't like our climate. And I cut them back and regrafted, and so it's continually evolving."

Today Stina and John grow eleven varieties of pears, twenty-five varieties of apples, and a few varieties of plums, apricots, peaches, and cherries. But still they spend the winter reading fruit catalogs, and they keep planting. "I just love planting trees!" says Stina, who admits there are challenges to growing so many different varieties. "They have different growth habits, and so they get pruned differently, they have certain nutritional requirements, and you have to figure out when to pick them all. It's actually kind of a royal headache. But it keeps it interesting."

And the more trees they plant, the more fruit there is to pick. The first year Stina realized, quite suddenly, that there are a lot of pears on an acre and a half. She had no access to a picking crew and hadn't met many locals yet, so she called up family and friends and said, "Hey, come pick pears! We'll have a party!" The result "was a disaster. We didn't have enough boxes and the fruit quality was quite poor, and we all came in from picking around six o'clock and scrambled around trying to make dinner, totally wrung out and tired."

The next year she got more organized. She asked a friend to cook for everyone and made sure there were plenty of boxes. Since then all the D'Anjous have been picked in an annual harvest party.

The other pear varieties Stina grafted in 2004, and just started to produce in 2009. They come off the trees sequentially, the way the apples do, which is part of the criteria used to choose them. The trick is to pick pears when they are mature but not ripe; you can't use taste as a sign of maturity. If pears are left on the tree too long, they get mushy at the core and rot from the middle out. If you want them to ripen evenly, you pick them green and rock hard. Pears are tested by pressure before picking, and each variety gets picked at a different pressure. It took a couple of seasons for Stina and John to figure out many of the older varieties. When they missed their windows, the fruit just fell to the ground.

"The apples are a little different, because we only have five to fifteen trees of each variety. They're big trees and they produce a lot, but they don't all come off at once the way the pears do." At some point Stina will need to hire pickers, but she loves the feeling of community she gets from her volunteer harvests, and is glad that she, John, and their friends can keep up with most of the day-to-day picking throughout the harvest season.

An iodine test helps them pick apples at their peak. As each variety gets close to its expected ripening date, they pick a few, cut them in half, and spray one half with an iodine solution. As the fruit matures, it converts starch to sugar. The iodine turns the starch black, creating a recognizable pattern on the fruit. They taste the other half of each apple for quality, but the iodine test gives them a clear visual indicator of how far along the fruit is in the starch-to-sugar conversion. It's particularly helpful because with so many varieties it can get confusing—some apples are more tart or taste more starchy than others. So they watch the results, give them numeric values, and write them down for next year.

Stina and John both love the rugged beauty of the hills and glacial landforms of the Twisp area. It was the outdoor recreation that brought each of them here (Stina from Seattle, and John from Ohio), so it's only appropriate that they met skiing. Neither seems to mind that the weather is extreme: very hot and dry in the summer and excruciatingly cold and dry in the

winter. They lost the last quarter of their 2009 crop to an early cold snap—one night in mid-October it dropped to 10 degrees Fahrenheit.

Harsh growing conditions have always plagued the Methow Valley; Stina describes it as fairly marginal fruit-growing country. The little pear orchard that started it all for her was planted in 1969 after the famous freeze of 1968, when it was minus-fifty for two weeks and most of the fruit trees in the valley were killed. Although her orchard got replanted, many did not. Apples and pears from the Methow used to get a premium because they pick later and grow in a cooler climate compared to the Wenatchee or Yakima Valleys, so they tend to store better. Coincidentally, the big freeze came at about the same time that controlled-atmosphere (CA) storage became available at an industrial level, where the oxygen is removed from the storage room, shutting down the metabolic processes in the fruit, enabling much longer storage times. "But after they come out of CA," Stina says, "they don't taste like anything at all."

Taste is paramount to Stina and John. Stina talks about the fruit coming from the thousand-acre industrial farms that used to grow just Fuji, Gala, and Braeburn, and are now growing more Honeycrisp, Zestar, and the next big things. "They all taste the same to me," she says. "Sweet and crisp and red. Which is fine. Honeycrisp is a nice apple. But there's just no comparison to a Prairie Spy or a Cox's Orange Pippin, which has all these flavors that go up your nose and down the back of your throat, and they're tremendously different and they look horrible. You can have a Honeycrisp that's nice, or you can have this flavor bomb. That's what we're trying to grow—the flavor bombs."

Because they grow all those "weird" varieties, Stina and John sell their fruit only at the farmers market. They cut up samples for tasting. "Otherwise they'd never sell," says Stina. "They're too ugly, they're too weird, they bruise too easily, they don't store well, people don't know what they are." Like the Egremont Russets: small and brown with green patches, they look like ugly potatoes. But fans fill bags with the sweet, richly flavored fruit and hoard them all winter.

There are other benefits to selling direct. Stina beams, "People love me! They love what I do! They'll come up to me and they'll look at my table and I've got thirteen different varieties out there and they'll say, 'Oh! I've never heard of any of them,' and so I give them a taste of each one and watch their face and they're like, 'Mmm, that was nice, and that's nice,' until you find one that just blows their doors and you can see it in their face, they're just like, 'Oh!' And I love that."

Both Stina and John also love the seasonality of farming. "Fall is super crazy and tense, but then it ends, and we get to recoup in the winter," Stina says. "And spring is super crazy and tense, in a different kind of way, but then we hit a lull in late summer. But what's daunting is that we are never actually done. There's never a day when we don't do something. Even in the dead of winter. And sometimes you just wish you could lie in bed all day and not get up.

"On the other hand," she says, smiling, "I get to work outside. I work for myself. I take my dogs to work. I work with living things. There's a lot of gratification and we do grow really wonderful fruit and it makes a lot of people really happy. It's a small thing, but it's worthwhile. And that's really good."

PIÑATA APPLE SALAD WITH HAZELNUTS AND CIDER GLAZE

Chef Jason Wilson of Crush Restaurant in Seattle uses Piñata apples (firm, juicy apples also known as Pinova or Sonata) for this salad. If you can't find them, just use a favorite variety. The apples, the concentrated cider glaze, and the complex flavors from the combination of greens make this salad all about Fall. You can use your favorite strong blue cheese here—a couple of Washington-made options include Willapa Hills Two-Faced Blue and Little Boy Blue.

1 cup Piñata apple juice or fresh apple cider

2 tablespoons apple cider vinegar

½ cup raw hazelnuts

3 tablespoons extra-virgin olive oil

3 tablespoons sherry vinegar

1 teaspoon Dijon mustard

¼ teaspoon kosher salt

¼ teaspoon freshly ground black pepper

2 Piñata apples, quartered and cored

2 cups fresh watercress, most of the stems removed

2 heads Belgian endive, cut crosswise into 1½-inch slices

1 cup frisée, torn

1 cup arugula leaves

2 tablespoons whole Italian parsley leaves

1 tablespoon chopped fresh sage

1 tablespoon fresh tarragon leaves

12 small slices prosciutto (2 to 3 ounces total)

3 ounces pungent blue cheese, crumbled

Preheat the oven to 350 degrees F.

To make the cider glaze, bring the apple juice and cider vinegar to a boil in a small saucepan over medium heat. Continue boiling until the mixture has reduced to about 3 tablespoons. (Be careful because it's not much and it burns easily.) Set the reduction aside.

Meanwhile, toast the hazelnuts on a baking sheet until they begin to color and smell nutty, about 12 minutes. Set them aside to cool, then roughly chop.

For the dressing, whisk together the olive oil, sherry vinegar, mustard, salt, and pepper, and set aside.

Slice the apples as thinly as you can (if you have a mandoline, this is the perfect job for it). Toss them with the watercress, endive, frisée, and arugula; add the parsley, sage, and tarragon, and dress with the vinaigrette. Divide the salad equally onto 6 plates and garnish with the hazelnuts, prosciutto, and blue cheese, then drizzle with the cider glaze.

MAKES 6 SERVINGS

CHESTNUT, APPLE, AND CELERIAC SOUP

Apples star in this decadently rich and creamy soup from Chef Bobby Moore of the Barking Frog restaurant in Woodinville. He likes to use Braeburns, Fujis, or Granny Smiths, depending on which variety is showing the most vibrant balance of sweet and tart notes. Not only is the garnish an elegant addition to the dish, but it adds textural contrast to the velvety smooth soup and an extra earthy note to its mildly sweet flavor.

1 pound vacuum-packed or individually quick-frozen (IQF) chestnuts

1 pound celeriac (also called celery root), peeled and cut into 1-inch chunks

1 pound apples (about 2 large), peeled and cored, cut into 1-inch chunks

About 2 cups water

About 2 cups heavy cream

⅓ cup plus 1 tablespoon honey, divided

Salt and white pepper

1 tablespoon unsalted butter

Before making the soup, set aside the components of the garnish. Put into a small bowl: 4 whole chestnuts, 3 chunks of celeriac, and 3 chunks of apple. Refrigerate until needed.

In a large heavy-bottomed saucepan, combine the remaining chestnuts, celeriac, and apple. Cover by 1 inch with equal amounts of water and cream. Bring to a boil very slowly, then reduce the heat to low. Cover the surface of the liquid with a piece of parchment paper cut to roughly fit the inside dimension of the pot. Simmer very gently for 2 hours (don't worry if the mixture begins to look curdled; just make sure it's at a very gentle simmer).

Remove the pot from the heat, discard the parchment, and use an immersion blender to purée the mixture until it is very smooth. Alternatively, transfer the hot mixture in batches to a food processor or blender and purée until smooth (use caution, as steam and hot liquids rise quickly in the processor and blender—just do a cup or two at a time). Return the purée to the pot and stir in ⅓ cup of the honey. Season to taste with salt and white pepper, then put the pot back on very low heat while you prepare the garnish.

Finely dice the reserved chestnuts, celeriac, and apple into ¼-inch cubes, keeping each separate. In a small sauté pan over medium heat, melt the butter and then add the celeriac and sauté until the edges begin to brown, about 2 minutes. Add the apple and sauté until it begins to soften, about 2 minutes more. Last, add the chestnut and sauté for another minute. Season lightly with salt and add the remaining 1 tablespoon of honey; mix so that the ingredients are well combined.

Ladle the soup into bowls and top each with a heaping tablespoon of the warm diced garnish.

MAKES 6 SERVINGS

MAKES 6 SERVINGS

CHICKEN LIVER MOUSSE CROSTINI
WITH PEAR RELISH

Chef Charlie Durham of Hudson Public House offers this recipe for an elegant hors d'oeuvre. He recommends using d'Anjou pears, and explains that the acidity of the pear relish cuts through the richness of the butter and takes advantage of the classic combination of pickled fruits with charcuterie. Since the relish keeps so well, Chef Durham suggests serving the leftover as a bright accompaniment to richer varieties of fish like salmon or black cod.

8 ounces chicken livers

¾ cup (1½ sticks) unsalted butter

1 tablespoon olive oil

¼ cup dry sherry

1 tablespoon honey

1 teaspoon salt

Freshly ground black pepper

1 fresh baguette

Pear Relish

2 large pears, ripe but still slightly firm

1 small shallot, minced

1 teaspoon minced fresh thyme

½ cup white wine vinegar

½ cup sugar

1 tablespoon whole grain mustard

Salt and freshly ground black pepper

Rinse the chicken livers and pat them dry with paper towels. Use a sharp knife to remove the stringy connective tissue. Cut the butter into ½-inch dice and refrigerate.

Heat a large skillet over high heat and add the olive oil. Sear the chicken livers until lightly browned on the outside but not cooked through, about 2 minutes on each side. Add the sherry and continue to cook, scraping the bottom of the pan with a spoon, until the wine has nearly evaporated. Transfer the livers to a food processor, add the cold butter, honey, salt, and a pinch of pepper and purée until smooth. Push the mousse through a fine-mesh strainer into a clean container. Press a piece of plastic wrap onto the surface of the mousse to keep the color from darkening, then cover the container tightly and refrigerate until the mousse is firm, at least 2 hours. If the mixture looks curdled after going through the strainer, move it to a bowl set over simmering water and whisk gently just until it looks smooth again, then transfer it to the container and refrigerate.

To make the relish, core the unpeeled pears and dice them into ¼-inch cubes (or as small as you can neatly dice them) and mix with the shallot and thyme in a small bowl. In a small saucepan, bring the vinegar, sugar, and mustard to a boil over medium-high heat, let cool for 1 minute, then pour over the pear mixture. Let the relish cool, stirring occasionally, then season it to taste with salt and pepper. The relish can be made up to one week ahead and kept refrigerated.

To serve, preheat the broiler. Drain the relish of any accumulated juices, reserving them in case you have leftover relish, and set it aside. Thinly slice the baguette on an angle and brush the top of each slice with a bit of olive oil. Spread the slices on a baking sheet and toast until the edges are just beginning to brown, about 2 minutes. Let the toasts cool before spreading them with the chicken liver mousse and topping each one with a table-spoon of well-drained relish.

MAKES 12 SERVINGS (ABOUT 1½ CUPS MOUSSE AND 3 TO 4 CUPS RELISH)

GINGER PEAR UPSIDE-DOWN CAKE

Rich and dark, this tender, moist cake from Chef Leslie Mackie, founder and driving force of Macrina Bakery & Cafe, smells heavenly and tastes even better. The pears cook slowly in the brown sugar caramel topping until they're soft as butter, while still holding their shape. You can find this and many more of Chef Mackie's amazing recipes in the Macrina Bakery & Cafe Cookbook.

Pear Layer

½ cup light brown sugar

3 tablespoons unsalted butter, at room temperature

1½ teaspoons cinnamon

4 to 5 ripe pears, peeled, cored, and quartered lengthwise

Cake

1 cup (2 sticks) unsalted butter, at room temperature

¾ cup light brown sugar

2 tablespoons peeled grated ginger

3 large eggs

⅔ cup mild molasses

3 cups all-purpose unbleached flour

1½ teaspoons baking powder

1½ teaspoons baking soda

½ teaspoon salt

1½ cups buttermilk

Preheat the oven to 325 degrees F. Oil a 10-inch springform pan and line the bottom with a circle of parchment paper. Set aside.

To make the pear layer, stir together the brown sugar, butter, and cinnamon in a medium saucepan over medium heat until the butter has melted and the mixture is smooth, about 2 minutes. Pour the mixture into the prepared pan, spreading it to completely cover the parchment circle. Place the quartered pears on top, arranging them slightly on edge, in a circle up against the sides of the pan; they will resemble the spokes of a wheel. Fill in the center of the circle with a couple of pear wedges. The pears should completely cover the bottom of the pan. Set the pan aside while you make the batter.

Cut the butter into 1-inch pieces and place in the bowl of a stand mixer. Add the brown sugar; using the paddle attachment, mix on medium speed for 5 to 8 minutes, until smooth and pale in color. Add the grated ginger, mix for another minute, and then scrape down the sides of the bowl with a rubber spatula. Add the eggs, one at a time, on low speed. Make sure each egg is fully incorporated before adding the next one. After the last egg is added, slowly add the molasses until it is well blended. The batter will look like it is breaking but it will come together when you add the dry ingredients. Remove the bowl from the mixer.

In a separate bowl, sift the flour, baking powder, baking soda, and salt. Alternate adding small amounts of the flour mixture and the buttermilk to the batter, mixing with a rubber spatula until each addition is well blended. Pour the batter into the springform pan, being careful not to dislodge the pears, and smooth the top.

Place the pan on a baking sheet (to catch any leaks) on the center rack of the oven. Bake the cake until a tester inserted in the center comes out clean, about 2 hours. Let the cake cool for 15 minutes. Run a thin knife all the way around the cake, reaching all the way to the bottom of the pan; invert it onto a serving dish. Release the catch and carefully remove the ring. Gently pry up the bottom of the pan and lift it off the cake. Carefully peel off the parchment circle, rearranging any pears that become dislodged in the process. Serve warm or at room temperature, by itself, or with whipped cream or ice cream.

MAKES 12 SERVINGS

APPLE JONNYCAKE COBBLER

This dessert from Pastry Chef Brittany Bardeleben of Crow and Betty restaurants combines a melting apple filling and a tender biscuit topping with a little cornmeal crunch. The extra steps she takes—making a syrupy apple cider reduction and sautéing the apples with nutty brown butter—make this apple cobbler a stand-out. Brittany suggests making the full recipe, which will feed a big, hungry crowd, in a deep ceramic lasagna dish—then eating the leftovers for breakfast! Note that the recipe calls for apple cider (not apple juice), as cider is unfiltered and still contains some apple pulp, which gives it a deeper, richer flavor. Rockridge Orchards in Enumclaw sells a variety of ciders at Seattle-area farmers markets.

2 cups unfiltered apple cider

5 pounds assorted apples (about 9 large)

Juice of 1 lemon (about 3 tablespoons)

½ cup sugar

¾ teaspoon cinnamon

¼ teaspoon grated nutmeg

⅛ teaspoon ground cloves

¼ teaspoon ground allspice

Pinch of salt

8 tablespoons (1 stick) unsalted butter

¼ cup Calvados or other apple brandy

Whipped cream or vanilla ice cream, for serving

Jonnycake Topping

1⅓ cups all-purpose flour

3 tablespoons sugar

⅓ cup stone-ground yellow cornmeal

2¼ teaspoons baking powder

¾ teaspoon salt

4 tablespoons (½ stick) cold, unsalted butter, cut into small cubes

1 cup plus 2 tablespoons heavy cream

Preheat the oven to 375 degrees F. Butter a large (9-by-12-inch) casserole or lasagna dish and set aside.

Pour the apple cider into a small pot and bring it to a boil. Cook until the cider has reduced to 1 cup. Keep a glass measuring cup nearby and from time to time measure the remaining cider. Strain and set aside.

Peel, core, and cut the apples into 1-inch chunks. Toss them with the lemon juice, sugar, cinnamon, nutmeg, cloves, allspice, and salt. In a pot or skillet large enough to hold all the apples, melt the butter over high heat. Continue to cook until the butter begins to brown and has a nutty aroma. Add the apples and let them sear for 2 to 3 minutes. Add the reduced cider. Bring to a simmer and reduce the heat to medium-low. Stir very gently, then cover with a lid or large piece of foil. Let the apples cook for 5 minutes. Turn off the heat, and let the apples sit, covered, for 5 more minutes. Pour the apples and all of the liquid from the skillet into the prepared baking dish and drizzle with the Calvados.

For the topping, combine the flour, sugar, cornmeal, baking powder, and salt in the bowl of a food processor fitted with the blade attachment. Pulse to combine. Add the butter and pulse until the mixture is crumbly and the butter is the size of small peas. Transfer the mixture to a large bowl; make a well in the center and add the cream. Mix, working quickly, with a wooden spoon until a soft biscuit dough forms. (You may need to add a few more tablespoons of cream to moisten all of the dry bits.) Do not overmix or the biscuits will be tough.

Use two spoons to drop the biscuit dough in coin-size pieces evenly onto the still-warm apples. Bake for 25 minutes, then reduce the oven temperature to 350 degrees F, rotate the pan, and continue baking until the biscuit is completely baked through, 10 to 15 minutes. It will be a very pale golden color with light brown edges and will feel firm to the touch. Serve warm with whipped cream or ice cream.

MAKES 12 SERVINGS

FORAGED FOODS

Mother Nature holds a monopoly on few foodstuffs these days. But we've yet to figure out how to domesticate delicacies like morels, truffles, and honey. Although our ancient ancestors survived for millennia as hunter-gatherers, both foraging and honey collecting are skills very few people in the United States still have. Most of us have absolutely no idea which wild foods are safe to eat—and as for bees, we see them and we run indoors!

Foraging requires many of the same skills as farming, but it can demand even more patience. Mushrooms are out there, or they aren't. Edible weeds are growing, or they're not. Wild foods can't be cultivated or covered with greenhouses; they can't be watered or fertilized. Foragers typically walk miles a day over vast amounts of rough terrain in hopes (not always realized) of finding their prizes. The bottom line is this: if the environment is healthy, it produces. The foragers who bring wild foods to our tables must be keenly attuned to nature and treat it with the utmost respect, because their livelihoods depend on it.

WILD THINGS

The Sound of Silence

Donna Westom was only three years old when she began accompanying her parents foraging around Arlington, Washington. They had a small farm, and Donna and her siblings worked hard milking cows and making butter; feeding the calves, pigs, and chickens; weeding the garden; stacking firewood; and when they were old enough, foraging. "They'd take me to the edge of where they were picking," she remembers, "and tell me to stand still." Not so that she wouldn't get lost, but rather so that she wouldn't step on anything edible. She was picking by the time she was four, but not eating. "I would never eat mushrooms when I was young. Not at all. Picking them was an Easter egg hunt! And it still is."

It's early October, and Donna sits in her regular spot at the University District Farmers Market behind a table piled high with golden orange chanterelles. Her long hair is tucked into a knitted cap, and her cold hands are tucked into the pockets of her corduroy jacket. When her cranky station wagon lets her, she drives down from Darrington, about eighty miles north of Seattle in the North Cascades, to sell whatever she's foraged. And although she calls her business Wild Things and sells wild mushrooms as well as weeds and berries, to many market regulars, she's "the Mushroom Lady."

For many years she foraged only for herself and her family. She worked in the lumber mill in Darrington and then in Marysville. In 1985 she applied for a business license, continuing to work at the lumber mill while on the side she foraged and sold what she found. "I was getting eight hours' sleep . . . a week," she laughs.

By the time her market table is groaning under its load of chanterelles, Donna's year is drawing to a close. She usually starts foraging for weeds in March when it's still extremely cold where she picks in the North Cascade mountains, and often she has to dig through new snow to find what she's looking for: stinging nettles, wood violets, miner's lettuce, and watercress. Mother Nature decides when she starts.

After the weeds come spring mushrooms: early morels, black morels, yellow morels, giant puffballs, Eastern spring coral, and porcini. Since Donna has foraged her whole life, she is absolutely sure of her mushroom identifications. In the areas she searches, there are a few kinds of poisonous mushrooms, but more that are edible than poisonous. "Usually they don't look anything like the ones you should pick. There's a couple that are kind of similar, but most of them that I pick you couldn't possibly mix up if you know what you're looking for."

Donna forages the same areas every season. In summer she picks wild blackberries, blackcaps, and red and blue huckleberries. In the fall she gathers chokecherries, elderberries, and a long list of mushrooms including chanterelle, porcini, lobster, Coral Hydnum, fried chicken, cauliflower, honey mushrooms, Matsutake, and chicken of the woods.

The best part of foraging for Donna is the peace. After ten years in the lumber mills, she was ready for some quiet. "I miss the guys at the mill" she says, but out in the woods, "there's no hollering and screaming, just the wind in the trees, birds singing, and squirrels barking."

When the mill was shut down and everyone laid off, Donna, along with many of her former co-workers, was sent to school for two years at Everett Community College. She already had her business license and knew her next career was going to be full-time foraging, but she did not get to choose her major—so to take the botany class she really wanted, Donna studied computers. She rolls her eyes. "They made me! I kept trying to tell them this is something I don't care about and I don't want to know. But I finally got my botany class!" At home in Darrington, Donna has no Internet connection, hence no e-mail address. Even her cell phone rarely works when she's out hunting, and never when she's at home—just the way she likes it.

The worst part of foraging for Donna is the weather. She often finds herself picking in snow in March, hundred-degree weather in August, and snow again in October. She knows she can't afford to wait for the weather to improve, because whatever she's hunting will be gone. "It's very stressful," she says. "You know there's weeds or berries or mushrooms out there so you've got to go, or go crazy knowing you missed the season."

Foraging is a solo activity. Once an area has been picked, there's nothing to do but wait until more comes up. So a forager like Donna, who makes her living selling what she finds, won't tell just anyone exactly where she hunts. A few areas are getting too difficult for her to access, so she's considering sharing them with others by giving classes. "I'm getting too old to keep them anymore," she says. "I might as well tell somebody. I can't take them with me."

Donna has been foraging many of the same spots her whole life (she helps ensure they're always producing by following her own golden rule: "Take some, leave some, give some away,

and give some back"). But there are edibles she has to keep a constant eye out for because their locations change. The little wild blackberries (her favorite foraged food) follow the loggers: two years after an area is clear-cut, the blackberries grow in profusion for just a few years until the new trees are about ten to fifteen feet tall, and then the berry plants die out from lack of sun.

It's the unpredictability of foraging that keeps her life interesting. Sometimes her patience gets tested. "You have to look hard for morels," she says. The dirt they grow in is just about the same color they are. And some days the foraging is easy. "I love it when I dream about where I need to pick that day," she says. "I don't know what road it's on, I can only see the forest, the logs to step over, the stumps with cauliflower, the logs with Hydnums, then I have to figure out which road those trees are on."

Although she occasionally sees other foragers when she's out hunting, more often Donna encounters animals. She's come across bears, cougars, coyotes, elk, bobcats, deer, and even a moose once. She carries a single-shot .22 rifle in her car for shooting Coral Hydnum out of the trees they grow in, but she's adamant that she'd never shoot an animal. When she sees one, she does nothing but watch them, because as she notes, the gun is vegetarian.

The oldest of four, Donna is the only one of her siblings who forages, and neither of her children has ever shown an interest. "They wouldn't remember where to go or what to pick," she says, shaking her head. "We used to go camping every weekend, and they'd swear they were being tortured." Of her three grandchildren, only one has ever shown an interest in foraging. His name is Jacob, and Donna is obviously happy to have his company. When she's shooting mushrooms out of trees, she usually puts a tarp down to catch them when they fall. But sometimes she can drop the gun fast enough to catch the mushrooms in her hands on their way down. Jake is impressed with these skills, and Donna gets a kick out of his reaction of, "Whoa, Grandma!"

On Donna's table sits an enormous binder of mushroom recipes. She spent a whole winter putting the book together, but her favorite way to eat mushrooms is simply sautéed in butter or bacon fat. She prefers the Coral Hydnum (a cream-colored clump that really does look like coral) and Morchella Escalante (a big yellow morel). Donna eats her fair share of chanterelles, to which she likes adding a little nutmeg and sometimes making them into a cream-based soup. Any mushrooms not sold fresh she takes home to dry (and then sells them dried at the market, too). She recommends grinding dried mushrooms, especially chanterelles, and using them to flavor just about anything.

As for berries, her weakness is the little blackberries. "I just sit there and eat the whole pail. Blackberries are the kind of thing that I can get the pail almost full and then I say, 'There's probably not enough to take home, let's just sit down and eat them.'" And she does, in the peace and quiet.

CHANTERELLE MUSHROOM RISOTTO

This creamy risotto from Chef Walter Pisano at Tulio Restaurant feels particularly luxurious because it's so packed with herb-infused, buttery chanterelles. Roasting the mushrooms intensifies their delicate flavor and adding them to the rice near the end of the cooking process keeps their texture firm.

1½ pounds chanterelle mushrooms

½ cup clarified unsalted butter*

1 clove garlic, smashed

5 thyme sprigs

5 sage leaves

¾ teaspoon salt

⅛ teaspoon white pepper

8 tablespoons (1 stick) unsalted butter, at room temperature, divided

1 medium white onion, finely diced

1 shallot, finely diced

1½ cups arborio rice

6 cups hot vegetable broth, plus more as needed

½ cup grated Parmesan cheese

6 tablespoons grated Pecorino Toscano cheese

Preheat the oven to 450 degrees F. To clean the mushrooms, wipe them carefully with slightly dampened paper towels; you may also need to use a paring knife to trim off parts that appear damaged. Leave the smaller ones whole and tear the large ones into several pieces. Put the clean mushrooms in a large bowl and set them aside. In a small saucepan, heat the clarified butter until it is hot but not smoking. Add the garlic, thyme, and sage, reduce the heat to low, and cook gently until the butter is infused with herb flavor, about 5 minutes. Strain the butter though a fine sieve over the mushrooms. Toss with the salt and pepper and spread out in a single layer on a baking sheet. Roast until the chanterelles are caramelized and tender, about 25 minutes, stirring occasionally.

While the mushrooms are roasting, melt 4 tablespoons of the butter in a heavy-bottomed saucepan over medium heat. Add the onion and shallot and stir constantly until softened, about 3 minutes. Add the rice and stir, coating and toasting the grains, for about 3 minutes more. Reduce the heat to keep the pot just at a simmer; add the vegetable broth one ladle at a time, stirring the rice constantly with a wooden spoon. Wait until almost all the liquid has been absorbed before adding the next ladleful. When the risotto is almost done, add the roasted chanterelles and mix well. This process should use about 6 cups of broth and take about 20 minutes.

To test the risotto for doneness, taste a few grains; the rice should have a firm bite, but should not be crunchy. If the risotto is not quite cooked, continue to add broth, adding very small amounts at a time. When the risotto is done, season to taste, then add the remaining

4 tablespoons butter and the Parmesan cheese. Spoon the risotto into serving bowls and garnish with the grated Pecorino cheese.

* When clarifying butter, you'll need to start with more than the amount called for in the recipe. Here, ½ cup (1 stick) plus 2 tablespoons should yield ½ cup clarified butter. Melt the butter slowly over low heat. Skim and discard the milk solids that float to the top, and then carefully pour the melted butter into a small dish, leaving behind the milk solids that sank to the bottom. The reserved liquid should be golden colored and clear.

MAKES 4 SERVINGS

GRANDVIEW MUSHROOM AND
CARAMELIZED ONION TARTS

Lisa Dupar, chef and owner of Lisa Dupar Catering and Pomegranate Bistro, shares this recipe for individual quiches. If you don't have small tart rings, you can also make this recipe using two 9-inch tart pans with removable bottoms—just increase the custard to 3 eggs and 1½ cups cream. Lisa gets her mushrooms from Kurt Hoenack's Grandview Mushrooms (hence the name). You can serve these tender little tarts warm from the oven, or cook up a batch of Lisa's tomato preserves (see page 19) and serve them, slightly warmed, on the side.

Tart Dough

2⅔ cups pastry flour (or substitute 2 cups all-purpose flour plus ⅔ cup cake flour)

1½ teaspoons kosher salt

1 cup (2 sticks) unsalted butter, cut into pieces, chilled

1½ teaspoons chopped fresh thyme

½ cup ice-cold water

Filling

2 tablespoons unsalted butter

2 cups thinly sliced white onions (about 1½ large onions)

3 tablespoons olive oil

3 cups roughly chopped assorted mushrooms (about 12 ounces)

2 large eggs

1 cup heavy cream

¼ teaspoon chopped garlic

Pinch of freshly grated nutmeg

½ teaspoon salt

⅛ teaspoon freshly ground black pepper

1 cup grated fontina or white cheddar cheese (about 3 ounces)

To make the tart shells, put the flour and salt into the bowl of a food processor and pulse to combine. Add the butter and thyme, and pulse until the butter is the size of peas. Add the water and pulse just until the dough begins to come together. Remove the dough from the bowl and squeeze it together to form it into a ball. Flatten the ball into a disk, wrap it well in plastic, and chill for at least 1 hour.

Take the dough out of the refrigerator and set it on your work surface to soften a little. Set eight 4-inch tart rings on a parchment-lined baking sheet. Roll the dough out on a lightly floured surface to ⅛-inch thickness. Cut the dough into 4 pieces and gently fit each piece into a ring. Use the back of a knife to trim the excess dough from the edges of the rings. Gather the dough scraps, roll them out again, and line the remaining rings. Chill the dough-lined rings for 20 minutes to minimize shrinkage during baking.

Preheat the oven to 350 degrees F. Cut parchment paper into pieces that are 6- to 7-inches square. Gently press a square into each of the unbaked tart shells, and fill them with pie weights or dried beans. Bake 20 minutes, then carefully lift the parchment paper (with the beans) out of the pastry shells. Continue baking the shells until they are golden brown, another 10 to 15 minutes (20 minutes for large tarts).

While the shells are baking, make the filling. Melt the butter in a large sauté pan over medium-low heat. Add the onions and sauté them, stirring often, until translucent, about 10 minutes. Increase the heat to medium and stir constantly until the onions are golden, about 10 minutes more. Transfer the onions to a large plate or bowl, add salt to taste, and set them aside to cool. Reheat the sauté pan over medium heat with the olive oil; add the mushrooms and sauté until limp and most of the liquid has evaporated, about 5 minutes. Season to taste.

In a medium bowl, whisk the eggs, then add the cream and whisk to blend. Add the garlic, nutmeg, salt, and pepper.

Divide the onions between the baked tart shells, then cover them with the mushrooms. Pour in the egg mixture, and then sprinkle each tart with cheese. Bake until the custard is set, 15 to 18 minutes (about 20 minutes for large tarts).

MAKES 8 SERVINGS

HERB-SCENTED BREAD PUDDING
WITH WILD MUSHROOMS

For her savory bread pudding at Volunteer Park Café, chef and co-owner Ericka Burke uses locally foraged mushrooms from Foraged & Found Edibles and brioche from Columbia City Bakery. Soft and creamy in the middle, crispy and crunchy on the top, the rosemary-scented pudding can be made ahead of time and reheated before serving.

Bread Cubes

1 loaf French bread or brioche (about 1 pound)

2 tablespoons unsalted butter

2 sage leaves, bruised by hand

1 small rosemary sprig, bruised by hand

Salt

Mushrooms

2 tablespoons olive oil

1½ teaspoons unsalted butter

½ medium yellow onion, cut into ¼-inch dice (about ½ cup)

1 tablespoon minced garlic

1½ pounds assorted mushrooms, preferably wild, cut into ½-inch pieces, divided

1½ teaspoons minced fresh rosemary

Salt and freshly ground black pepper

Custard

3 large eggs

1 egg yolk

1 cup heavy cream

1½ teaspoons minced fresh rosemary

1 teaspoon minced fresh sage

1½ teaspoons porcini mushroom powder (optional)

½ teaspoon salt

⅛ teaspoon freshly ground black pepper

Preheat the oven to 350 degrees F. Cut the bread into ½- to 1-inch cubes and place in a large mixing bowl. You should have at least 7 generous cups of cubed bread. Melt the butter in a small saucepan over medium heat. Add the sage and rosemary, reduce the heat to low, and cook for about 5 minutes, allowing the herbs to infuse the butter with their flavors. Remove the herbs and discard them, then pour the butter over the cubed bread and toss well to coat. Season to taste with salt. Spread the bread cubes out onto a baking sheet and toast them in the oven until slightly crisp, about 20 minutes, stirring once or twice while they bake.

For the mushrooms, heat the olive oil and butter in a large sauté pan over medium heat. Add the onion and garlic and sauté gently until aromatic, 1 to 2 minutes. Add half the mushrooms and the rosemary, and sauté until the mushrooms start to shrink and release their natural juices, 2 to 3 minutes, then add the remaining mushrooms. Sauté until all the mushrooms become limp and have released most of their juices, 7 to 10 minutes more. Season to taste with salt and pepper.

To make the custard, whisk the eggs, egg yolk, cream, rosemary, sage, mushroom powder, salt, and pepper together until smooth. Set aside.

Combine 6 cups of the toasted bread (if there's any leftover you can toast them a little longer and use them as salad croutons) and sautéed mushrooms (with any residual juices) in a large mixing bowl. Add the custard and stir to mix well. Let the mixture stand for 30 minutes, stirring gently once or twice to ensure that the custard is being absorbed. Put the mixture in an 8-by-10-inch baking dish. Cover the pan with foil and bake until the custard is set, about 50 minutes. The custard is set when the bread in the center is no longer wet and springs back when pressed. Remove the foil, return the pudding to the oven, and bake until the top is pale golden, about 10 minutes more.

MAKES 6 SERVINGS

CEDAR PLANK–ROASTED WILD MUSHROOMS

Roasting wild mushrooms with lemon and herbs accentuates their richness and adds a bright note that makes this side dish from Chef John Howie and his Seastar restaurants the perfect accompaniment to anything from roast chicken to grilled meats; or you can toss them with your favorite pasta and cheese for a satisfying vegetarian dish. Roasting on a cedar plank, one of Chef Howie's signature techniques, imparts a smoky flavor to the food.

2½ pounds assorted wild mushrooms,* cleaned and roughly chopped into 2-inch pieces

¾ cup olive oil

2 tablespoons freshly squeezed lemon juice, plus 6 thin lemon slices for garnish

1 tablespoon "3 Chefs in a Tub" Porcini Mushroom Rub (recipe follows)

1 teaspoon minced garlic

2 teaspoons minced fresh thyme, plus 6 small sprigs for garnish

½ teaspoon minced fresh rosemary, plus 6 small sprigs for garnish

½ teaspoon minced fresh sage, plus 6 small sprigs for garnish

½ teaspoon kosher salt

¼ teaspoon freshly ground black pepper

Preheat the oven to 425 degrees F.

In a large bowl, toss the mushrooms with the olive oil, lemon juice, mushroom rub, garlic, minced thyme, minced rosemary, minced sage, salt, and pepper until well coated. Spread the mushrooms on a cedar plank and bake for about 20 minutes, until the edges are golden. (If you don't have a cedar plank, you will still get very good results roasting the mushrooms on a baking sheet.) Taste for seasoning, then serve, garnished with the lemon slices and herb sprigs.

* If wild mushrooms are not available, you can substitute 1 pound of portobello mushroom caps (cut into 1½-inch chunks) plus 1 pound crimini mushrooms (halved) plus 8 ounces shiitake mushrooms (stems removed, cut into large pieces).

MAKES 6 SERVINGS AS A SIDE DISH

"3 Chefs in a Tub" Porcini Mushroom Rub

Chef John Howie's rub is pure concentrated flavor. Once you've got it in your kitchen, you'll find many uses for it. It's also available ready-made from www.plankcooking.com.

2 ounces dried porcini mushrooms

¼ cup plus 2 tablespoons sea salt

2 tablespoons plus 2 teaspoons finely minced lemon zest (from about 4 lemons)

1 tablespoon plus 1 teaspoon dried thyme

1 teaspoon ground white pepper

Place the dried porcinis in the bowl of a food processor and pulse until powdered. Add the salt, lemon zest, thyme, and pepper, and pulse until the mixture is finely ground. Transfer to an airtight container and store at room temperature.

MAKES 1½ CUPS RUB

BROWN BUTTER POLENTA CAKES WITH FIDDLEHEAD FERNS

Executive Chef Craig Hetherington shares this recipe, a TASTE Restaurant fan favorite, featuring Samish Bay gouda. The decadent, cheesy polenta cakes show off the bright spring flavors of foraged fiddleheads and sweet, freshly shelled peas.

7 tablespoons unsalted butter, divided

2 cups half-and-half

2 tablespoons chopped fresh thyme

2 tablespoons chopped fresh sage

¼ teaspoon chili flakes

½ cup coarse cornmeal (polenta), preferably stone-ground

1 cup shredded Samish Bay gouda (about 3½ ounces)

Salt and freshly ground black pepper

2 tablespoons olive oil, divided

1 cup heavy cream

2 cups fiddlehead ferns

1 cup shelled English peas (or substitute frozen peas)

Lightly oil an 8-inch-square baking dish and set aside.

Melt 6 tablespoons of the butter in a medium heavy-bottomed saucepan over medium heat and cook until the butter bubbles, the milk solids just start to turn brown, and the butter smells nutty, about 4 minutes. Carefully pour in the half-and-half, then add the thyme, sage, and chili flakes; increase the heat to medium-high and bring to a boil. Reduce the heat to medium and, whisking constantly with a wire whisk, add the cornmeal in a steady stream (this keeps the polenta from sticking to the bottom of the pan and getting lumpy). Once the polenta has been added, reduce the heat to low and cook, stirring occasionally, until the polenta has absorbed all of the liquid and the cornmeal is no longer crunchy. Check the instructions on the bag as cooking times can vary significantly by brand and the coarseness of the cornmeal. Once the polenta is done, increase the heat to medium and add all of the cheese at once. Stir until the cheese has completely melted. Season to taste with salt and a couple of grinds of pepper. Pour the polenta into the prepared pan. Let cool, uncovered (you want a slight skin to form), in the refrigerator for 2 to 3 hours or overnight. Use a round cookie cutter or a knife to cut the polenta into 6 pieces.

Just before serving, preheat the oven to 250 degrees F. Add 1 tablespoon of the olive oil to a large sauté pan over medium heat. When the oil is hot, sauté the polenta cakes, top side down, until lightly golden, about 2 minutes. Turn the cakes over, reduce the heat to medium-low and continue to cook until the other side is nicely brown and the center is heated through, another 3 to 4 minutes. Keep the cakes warm in the oven until ready to serve.

Put the cream in a small saucepan over medium heat and simmer to reduce it to ⅓ cup. Cover to keep warm.

In a clean sauté pan, heat the remaining 1 tablespoon each olive oil and butter over medium-high heat. Add the fiddleheads and peas and quickly sauté, about 3 minutes (the vegetables should still be a little crunchy). Season to taste with salt and pepper.

To serve, place a polenta cake on each plate. Drizzle the cream around it. Put the vegetables on top of the cake and serve right away.

MAKES 6 SERVINGS

WILD HUCKLEBERRY PIE

Heather Earnhardt, chef and co-owner of Volunteer Park Café, just can't wait for huckle-berry season to come around every autumn. "It's short but sweet," she observes. Heather loves the floral aroma and intense, concentrated flavor of the dark purple berries, and appreciates that they are smaller and more difficult to harvest than their domesticated cousins, blueberries. "I try to keep that in mind and give the berries the respect they deserve." Foraged & Found Edibles picks loads of wild huckleberries each year and pro-vides them to many restaurants in the Seattle area, including Volunteer Park Café.

Pie Dough

2 cups (10 ounces) unbleached all-purpose flour

2 tablespoons granulated sugar

1 teaspoon kosher salt

½ cup (1 stick) plus 2 tablespoons unsalted butter, diced, frozen

4 egg yolks

¼ cup ice-cold water, plus more as needed

1 large egg, beaten with 2 teaspoons water

1½ teaspoons turbinado sugar

Huckleberry Filling

2 pounds fresh or frozen wild huckleberries

½ cup granulated sugar

3 tablespoons instant tapioca or cornstarch

1 lemon, zested and juiced (about 2 teaspoons zest and 3 tablespoons juice)

To make the dough, put the flour, sugar, and salt in the bowl of a food processor fitted with the blade attachment; pulse to combine. Add the frozen butter and pulse until the butter is in pieces the size of very small peas. Add the egg yolks and pulse a couple of times to com-bine. Add the ice water and pulse a few times, just until the dough starts clumping together. Squeeze a bit of the dough to check if it is holding together; add more ice water, a teaspoon at a time, if necessary. Divide the dough in half, form each half into a ball, flatten them into disks, and wrap them in plastic. Refrigerate for 1 hour.

While the dough is chilling, make the huckleberry filling by tossing the huckleberries, sugar, tapioca, lemon juice, and lemon zest together in a large bowl. Set aside.

Have a pie dish ready. Roll out one portion of the dough on a lightly floured surface to a circle at least 13 inches in diameter, and no more than ¼ inch thick. Lay the crust into the pie dish with the excess dough hanging over the sides. Fill with the huckleberry filling. Brush the edges of the dough with a little of the beaten egg. Roll out the other portion of dough to a large circle no more than ¼ inch thick and drape it on top of the filling. Trim the dough (a clean pair of scissors works well) so that it extends over the edge of the pie dish by about an inch. Roll the edges of the dough under and pinch gently to seal the two pieces together. Then crimp decoratively if desired. Cut several slits in the top of the pie to let steam escape.

Brush the full surface of the pie with the beaten egg and sprinkle with the turbinado sugar. Freeze until solid. (Freezing the pie before baking helps ensure a crisp bottom crust, as it will start baking before the filling liquefies. If you're not going to bake the pie within 24 hours, wrap well once it's frozen and keep frozen until ready to bake.)

When you're ready to bake the pie, preheat the oven to 375 degrees F. Put a baking sheet on the rack beneath the pie to catch the buttery drips. Bake in the center of the oven until the crust is a deep golden brown and the fruit is bubbling, about 1 hour and 15 minutes. (If the outside edges of the piecrust are getting too brown, set a ring of aluminum foil loosely on the edges to protect them.) Let the pie cool on a rack before slicing it.

Serve the pie with vanilla ice cream or lightly sweetened whipped cream. If you like the pie filling loose, serve the pie warm or at room temperature; if you prefer the filling set, serve it cold.

MAKES 8 GENEROUS SERVINGS

TAHUYA RIVER APIARIES

— The Bee Man of the Olympics —

When Roy Nettlebeck was a little boy, he'd sit on his grandfather's lap every Sunday and listen to him read from *National Geographic*. When he was five, his grandfather read him a piece about life in a beehive. "It was fascinating. Unbelievable. A colony, one unit, that you can look at and see just about everything you would ever want to see. And thousands and thousands of different evolutions going on to sustain itself, and it's been doing that for 30 million years." That day he told his grandfather, "Someday I'm going to have honeybees."

Little Roy grew up, served two tours in Vietnam, and got a job at the naval shipyard in Bremerton. As soon as he'd saved enough to buy property, he bought bees and equipment from Sears & Roebuck. "Of course, I started off on the wrong foot. I had bees up in the trees two hours after I put them in the box! I didn't read far enough in the book." Even though he had two books, both considered bibles for beekeepers, they continually contradicted each other, so Roy decided to let the bees teach him themselves.

After thirty-two years at the shipyard, Roy took early retirement, and beekeeping went from a hobby to his full-time occupation. He was fifty-two years old and had always felt passionately about the bees—honey was merely a sideline. "Bees are number one for me. I take care of the bees, and they may take care of me with some honey or they may not, but I'm going to take care of them." When Roy refers to the bees, he calls them "the girls."

Roy had studied chemistry and went through nuclear power school in the navy. In order to better understand his bees and bee genetics, he studied biology on his own. His connection to his bees is very visceral. "Everything in the universe works on wavelengths," he explains. "Communication is not just sound, but also you're looking at me and I'm looking at you. And some people we have a good rapport with, and we don't even know them from squat. There's just something we feel about them. That's why there are 'bee havers' and 'beekeepers.' Beekeepers are capable of going into that space with the honeybee. I lift a lid on a beehive and I disappear." Roy covers up with a bee suit when he'll bang frames around and pull honey, but otherwise he is calm and relaxed, and the bees aren't afraid.

In August 2009, after forty-seven years, Roy reconnected with Pat Slaten, his girlfriend from high school. They had lost touch when he'd joined the navy and she left home to work for Volunteers in Service to America (VISTA). Kindred spirits, they now work together taking care of the bees. Roy keeps some of his eighty hives on Pat's Sweetwater acreage 1,200 feet up in the Olympic Mountains overlooking Port Angeles, and others at his Tahuya River apiary on Hood Canal. The rest are at various Forest Service locations throughout the Olympics.

Pat, who's embraced the beekeeping life as though it was always meant to be, helps Roy organize his notes and keep track of the health of and activity in his hives. Although worker bees live only thirty to fifty days in the summer, and at most six months over the winter, queens can live for a couple of years. A queen bee lays between one thousand and fifteen-hundred eggs a day. If the eggs are healthy, they all hatch—so a normal hive expands very quickly. Bees keep their hives at a remarkably constant 92 degrees F. When it's cold outside, the population inside the hive is allowed to grow so that the bees' body heat can keep it warm. When it's hot, the bees keep the hive cool by bringing water that evaporates and cools the air inside and by fanning their wings to keep air moving. But when the population grows too large, the bees either need more room (a beekeeper would add another box to the hive's tower) or some of them must move out. In an overcrowded hive, scout bees fly off to find new space. When they return, they release a pheromone that excites the old queen and about half the population to leave. The huge clump of relocating bees is called a swarm.

Over the summer, Roy stored a tower of empty bee boxes outside his cozy whitewashed log cabin in Port Angeles, with plans to take them up to Pat's place. Even though he's been keeping bees for more than forty years, Roy's voice fills with wonder as he recounts the day a swarm moved in: "I saw the scouts out there. I knew something was going on, but I didn't know if they were going to bless it. But then two hours later all hell broke loose! I started hearing such a noise. I opened up the door and it was yellow with bees. I shut it and I called Pat and I said 'Hey, you know that box in the back? We won't have to move it!'"

Roy keeps his bees far from conventional agriculture because he doesn't want them pollinating and collecting nectar from plants that have been sprayed or treated in any way. And while that makes his honey pure and healthy for human consumption, what's more important to him is that it keeps his bees healthy.

All over North America and Europe, the honeybee population has been disappearing at a rapid, worrisome rate. "*Apis mellifera* is an environmental indicator species," Roy says. In his eyes, that they appear to be in trouble is a sign that the whole planet is in trouble. (One of the most popular theories to explain the population's decline points to the *Varroa* mite, which has developed resistance to all the chemical treatments created to destroy it. It infects honeybees with a number of viruses, some of which have been around for a long time, while others were more recently introduced by imported bees. Because bees are such social creatures, the viruses spread quickly and the hives collapse. Other theories blame environmental change–related stresses and the use of pesticides.)

Lately, Roy has focused his attention on raising bees that are naturally resistant to the devastating viruses. Last year he lost no hives, a success he attributes to leaving ten of them at four thousand feet in the Olympic Mountains through the winter. Thirty percent of the bees survived, and he used those as breeding stock, using natural selection for the strongest and the fittest. Roy watches hive populations closely to avoid inbreeding, which has a detrimental effect on egg and larvae viability. He also uses an organic approach to nutrition: before the bees start gathering nectar, he feeds them a sugar syrup with peppermint oil, lemongrass oil, and colloidal silver—all natural antibacterials and antivirals.

In the story *The Bee Man of Orn*, a beekeeper who looks suspiciously like Roy (white hair curling at the nape of his neck, full white beard and mustache) lives a long, full life and gets the chance to do it all over differently, but instead he chooses to be a beekeeper again. Listening to Roy talk about bees, his language alternating between scientific and poetic, it is obvious that he'd choose bees again, too.

Roy's eldest son Josh runs their website (www.hiveharvest.com), works the University District Farmers Market on Saturdays, and helps Roy extract honey when he's not caring for his own family; son-in-law Ben works the Sunday Ballard Market and is also a stay-at-home dad. Roy's daughter, Molly, speaks six languages and has a Master's degree from the University of Washington; his youngest son, Ian, is in the National Guard, having recently returned from serving in Afghanistan. When Roy talks about his family, you can hear the pride and love in his rough voice.

On a hot, dry day near the end of summer, Roy took me to visit some of his bees. I was carefully covered from head to toe in a white bee suit with a screened hood around my head, neck, and chest, plus long gloves with elastic to hold tightly to my upper arms. A dozen hives in varying shades of green stood in two neat rows. From twenty feet you could see bees flying in and out of the bottom-most box of each hive, but it was the sound that was incredible—a high-pitched screaming. It was terrifying to think about just how many bees it takes to make so much noise. But as we got closer, the bees were so busy they ignored us. It took only a moment to go from panic mode to admiration. They were plump and fuzzy; little golden teddy bears with wings.

I tried to lift a box from one of the hives, but it barely budged. Sweat already dripped down the inside of my suit. Sixty-eight-year-old Roy lifted the ninety-pound box, turned, and placed it gently on a board before reaching for the next one. Stepping slowly and purposefully, careful not to step on even one bee, he checked inside each box, looking for eggs and larvae and to see how full of honey the frames were and whether the comb was capped. Startlingly clear fireweed honey dripped from the comb he gently extricated from a box. He cut a chunk and dropped it into a bucket. Not a single bee had even been injured.

Later we stood in the quiet shade and chewed the cool, sweet honey out of the soft comb. I tried to appreciate that a bee flies 55,000 miles to produce one pound of honey, and that all over the world millions of bees are always working. Roy told me that three thousand years ago, the Egyptians put honey in King Tut's tomb, and recent scientific analysis showed no degradation whatsoever. "I can't think of a more wonderful product to be involved with," he said, chewing thoughtfully.

HONEY-MARINATED SALMON WITH WALNUTS AND CRANBERRIES

Chef Charlie Durham of Hudson Public House shares his recipe for this vibrant dish that's perfect for a dinner party, because everything can be prepared ahead; just cook the salmon at the last minute. The honey serves to accentuate the natural sweetness of the salmon, while herbs and tangy cranberries balance its richness.

Dressing

½ cup strongly flavored honey, divided

¼ cup canola oil

2 tablespoons white wine vinegar

2 tablespoons minced thyme leaves

2 tablespoons minced Italian parsley

2 tablespoons minced shallot

1 tablespoon minced garlic

1 teaspoon kosher salt

½ teaspoon freshly ground black pepper

⅛ teaspoon cayenne pepper

Salmon

4 wild salmon fillets (about 6 ounces each), skin off, pin bones removed

1 cup walnut halves

Salt

1 cup fresh or frozen cranberries (thawed and drained)

2 tablespoons olive oil

1 small head butter lettuce, leaves washed, dried, and torn

To make the dressing, combine ¼ cup of the honey, the oil, vinegar, thyme, parsley, shallot, garlic, salt, black pepper, and cayenne in a blender and purée until smooth. Put ¼ cup of the dressing in a small bowl and whisk in the remaining ¼ cup honey to make the salmon marinade. Set the rest of the dressing aside. Brush the marinade onto the salmon and let it sit, covered, for 2 hours in the refrigerator.

Preheat the oven to 325 degrees F. Cover the walnuts with water in a small pot, bring to a simmer, and then drain. Lightly salt the walnuts and then spread them on a baking sheet with the cranberries. Roast until the nuts are fragrant and the cranberries are soft, about 15 minutes. Set aside.

Heat a large, nonstick ovenproof skillet over medium-high heat. Lift the salmon fillets from the marinade and shake off the excess, then season lightly with salt. Add the olive oil to the skillet and place the fish skin side up in the pan. Let the fish brown lightly, about 3 minutes, turn the pieces over, and put the skillet into the oven. Roast until the fish is cooked to your liking (about 1 minute for medium, up to 4 minutes for well done). Remove the skillet from the oven, and then transfer the fillets to a plate to rest. Tent lightly with foil to keep warm.

Reserve 2 tablespoons of the dressing for garnish. Toss the lettuce with the remaining dressing and divide it between the plates. Place the salmon on the lettuce and top with the cranberries and walnuts. Finish with a drizzle of the dressing.

MAKES 4 SERVINGS

HONEY-SOY-CURED PACIFIC MACKEREL WITH HOT MUSTARD

Seattle chef and restaurateur Tom Douglas serves an array of flavorful fish and seafood appetizers like this one at Dahlia Lounge called "Little Tastes of the Sea Bar." For this dish, he gets his Pacific mackerel and "ocean salad" (prepared seaweed dressed with sesame oil and rice vinegar) from Mutual Fish and his honey from Hivemind honey, both Seattle-based businesses. The intensely flavored cure quickly permeates the fish and firms up the texture, so it's best to marinate for no more than 8 hours. Although the recipe calls for one fillet, you'll end up with 2 if you buy a whole fish. Marinate and grill the second fillet, too, because leftovers are delicious flaked and served on a salad, with baby steamed potatoes, or any way you usually enjoy smoked fish.

½ cup soy sauce

¼ cup plus 2 tablespoons honey

2 tablespoons water

2 tablespoons sake

1 tablespoon chopped garlic

1 teaspoon grated fresh ginger

1 scallion, white and light green parts only, chopped

¼ orange, thinly sliced

One 6- to 8-ounce Pacific mackerel fillet, skin on

1 teaspoon sesame seeds

1 tablespoon ocean salad

Hot Mustard

2 tablespoons dry hot mustard

1½ teaspoons rice wine vinegar

1½ teaspoons soy sauce

Combine the soy sauce, honey, water, and sake in a bowl and stir to blend. Add the garlic, ginger, scallion, and orange slices. Put the mackerel in a non-reactive pan and pour the marinade over it. Cover tightly with plastic wrap and refrigerate for about 8 hours.

Put the sesame seeds in a small heavy skillet over medium heat and toast them, stirring constantly, until they are light brown. Set aside.

To make the mustard, add water to the mustard powder, 1 teaspoon at a time, to make a thick paste, then add the vinegar and soy sauce; whisk until smooth. Set aside.

To cook the mackerel, preheat a charcoal or gas grill and oil the grates. Remove the mackerel from the marinade and shake off the excess. Grill the fillet over medium-high heat, skin side down, until the skin begins to curl at the edges, 2 to 3 minutes. (Watch carefully to make sure it doesn't burn.) Use a metal spatula to carefully turn the fillet over; grill until cooked through, 2 to 3 minutes more. To serve, cut the fish into 4 pieces, and garnish each with some of the sesame seeds and the ocean salad. Serve with the hot mustard on the side.

MAKES 4 APPETIZER SERVINGS

HONEY SEMIFREDDO

This frozen honey mousse from Dana Cree, former pastry chef at Poppy, really showcases the flavor of the honey, so choose a honey you love—preferably from a local beekeeper you love! Serve it simply with a sprig of mint, a drizzle of dark chocolate sauce, or fresh berries for a perfect cool, easy summer dessert.

⅓ cup honey (4 ounces)

2 egg yolks

Seeds from ½ vanilla bean

1½ cups heavy cream, cold

Prepare a 9-by-5-inch loaf pan by moistening it with a damp towel and then lining it with plastic wrap or foil; alternatively, prepare a muffin tin with 10 cupcake liners. Set aside.

Make a double boiler by choosing a metal bowl large enough to fit over a pot filled with about 2 inches of simmering water (do not let the bottom of the bowl touch the water). Whisk the honey, egg yolks, and vanilla seeds together in the bowl until well blended. Keeping the water at a gentle simmer, whisk the honey mixture vigorously and constantly until it is thick and pale, 5 to 10 minutes. The mixture is cooked when a stream drizzled back into the bowl leaves a trail rather than disappearing right away. Remove the bowl from the pot and allow the mixture to cool until just barely warm to the touch.

Meanwhile, whip the cream to soft peaks. Before continuing, make sure that the cream is cold and the honey mixture is just barely warm. If it is too warm, the honey mixture will melt the cream rather than combine with it.

Add one third of the cream to the honey mixture and blend together until smooth. Add the remaining cream and fold together gently. Pour the mousse into the prepared pan or molds, cover with plastic wrap (making sure the plastic touches the mousse), and store in the freezer for at least 8 hours or overnight.

When ready to serve, note that the semifreddo will be easier to slice and will hold its form better if you chill both the cutting board and the individual dessert plates before serving. Use the plastic wrap to lift the semifreddo from the loaf pan; peel off the plastic and slice it with a clean, sharp knife into pieces about 1 inch thick. You can run the knife under hot water and dry it between slices for a neater, more beautiful presentation. Place one slice on each chilled plate and garnish as desired. For the cupcake shapes, peel off the paper and serve upside down.

MAKES 10 SERVINGS

WINE

In 1981 there were only nineteen wineries in the state of Washington. Twenty years later there were 170, and in 2010 there were more than 700. Wine grapes are our state's fourth largest fruit crop—we grow about 150,000 tons on 37,000 acres.

Our wine industry is growing rapidly, and Washington is currently the second largest wine-producing state, after California. Although this sounds impressive, California accounts for 90 percent of US wine production. John Bookwalter helped put this in context by noting that we grow fewer grapes in the whole state of Washington than they grow just chardonnay grapes in the Burgundy wine region of France. So although Washington wines take up a lot of shelf space here, the 12 million cases we produce each year make up just a tiny percentage of the world's wine. But what we lack in quantity, we more than make up for in quality. Washington wines are highly acclaimed by critics all over the world.

There are eleven Washington wine appellations, most in the arid central and southern regions of the state. Washington grape growers and winemakers are committed to sustainable agriculture and water conservation, and their wine grapes have proven not only to be an economically viable crop that flourishes on difficult terrain with little water but also to produce remarkably fine wines.

CADARETTA

Branching Out

In 1898, Rick Middleton's great-grandfather came from Michigan to Washington with his father-in-law to start a forestry products company. More than a century later, Anderson & Middleton still thrives in Hoquiam. The company's history is a living example of how being willing to try new things is key to the survival of a family business. Cadaretta winery in Walla Walla is the newest piece of the business, and while it might surprise Rick's great-grandfather, it came about quite naturally.

Anderson & Middleton still harvests timber for sawmills, but they no longer mill lumber. Their last manufacturing company was called Grays Harbor Veneer, also based in Hoquiam. The company made boxes for the tree fruit and table grape industries in California, but by the early 1990s, those boxes were being replaced by less expensive ones made of corrugated cardboard or Styrofoam. The family left the business, but not before moving part of their operations to Delano, California, in the San Joaquin Valley, to be closer to their customers. Looking to diversify out of forest products, and already running an office in Delano, the Middletons began farming table grapes. That business has grown so much in the last twenty years that it's the largest part of the company.

About ten years later, the family decided to diversify again, and the natural progression was to wine grapes. They purchased land in Paso Robles, on the central coast of California, and were soon selling to a large portfolio of winemakers. "It's a slippery slope, once you start growing wine grapes," Rick laughs,

"someone's going to want to make wine." For a few years they made wine for fun and gave it all away; in 2003 they started Clayhouse Vineyard and produced their first vintage.

That same year, Rick and his family took a trip over to Walla Walla with their consulting winemaker. "We're from Washington, we all live up here, we're fans of wine. And we really liked what was going on in the wine industry in the Pacific Northwest," Rick explains.

In 2005, the Middletons purchased property in the Walla Walla Valley. The land was surrounded by well-known vineyards, so it wasn't a hard decision and didn't take any great skill on their part, Rick admits. The family took the new winery very seriously. "We made the decision early on that we wanted to be methodical. This wasn't stuff we should rush on. We knew we wanted to go for very high-end products, and we wanted to take our time and try to get it right and really understand what we have."

Cadaretta's land is complex. The elevation rises from 950 to about 1,400 feet. At the lower elevation the soil is quite deep, but at the top it is thin and rocky. Wheat was grown there for thirty years, so the soil was depleted. They decided it made sense to study the land, learn where all the variations were, the differences in the soil, the aspect and exposure to the sun and wind. It was an expensive proposition, but the more prepared they were, the fewer mistakes they'd make.

After two years studying, they began to improve the land, growing green manure crops, tilling them into the soil, and installing irrigation. The first vines were planted on twenty-two acres in 2008. It takes about three years to produce the first crop, and Cadaretta plans to start playing around with the fruit in year four. But aiming for a high-end product, Rick estimates it will be seven or eight years before they really rely on their own fruit production.

"We've planted a lot of different varietals of grapes," Rick says. "Some that we have a really high confidence in. And then we have others that are really an acre of this and an acre of that—we want to see how it does on the site." Rick feels good about the chances for his cabernet and other Bordeaux varietals, and some of the Rhone varietals like syrah, based on what he's tasted from his neighbors. He is more curious and anxious about grenache, mourvedre, and sangiovese, among others. "There's opportunity for phenomenal fruit," he says.

Cadaretta produces their wines in a facility in the town of Walla Walla, and for now sources fruit mostly from vineyards in the Walla Walla Valley. Rick is clear that he owes much of their early success to the Washington wine industry, and to the Walla Walla Valley in particular. "It's such a supportive group of people," he says, "very welcoming." He's well aware that there are lots of places in Washington to grow grapes and make great wine, but "what makes Walla Walla particularly special to me is its excellent people. There's a real town there, with a rich history based on wheat and other crops, a world class liberal arts college, a great community college. There was a real community there before wine ever happened."

Rick understands the significance of history—he's as much a product of his family history as Cadaretta is. Growing up, he worked at Anderson & Middleton during the summers while attending the University of Washington. He was so familiar with the family business that when he decided to do something different after five years working as a foreign services officer for the U.S. State Department, it was natural to come back.

His children are still young, and Rick doesn't yet have any idea if they'll want to be involved in the business. He works with his sister and a number of cousins, so the company still feels like a family business to him, four or five generations in—and he hopes it will continue that way.

Rick sees wine as an important part of the company's future, noting how different it is from the rest of the company. "Selling logs to a sawmill—it's the ultimate commodity," he says. Table grapes are somewhere in between. "It seems like a commodity, but your reputation is everything." And then there's the wine. "It's interesting because you've got to have a great product, but at the end of the day you have to have someone choose to buy your product."

But long before anyone can choose to buy a bottle of Cadaretta, "Someone has to be a good farmer and the grapes have to be stellar. Then someone has to be stellar in the winery. And then the real heavy lifting begins because then you have to be able to communicate your story and your passion so that someone wants to buy it." Listening to Rick talk about Cadaretta, it's apparent that one of the things he loves best about his job is seeing how customers respond to his wines. In Anderson & Middleton's other businesses there isn't the same opportunity to meet the consumer.

Cadaretta is named for one of the company's ships from the 1920s and '30s that carried timber from Washington to California. Rick and his family are proud of their history; naming the winery Cadaretta is one way they've chosen to honor it. Rick's plan for Cadaretta's future is "to be thoughtful about what we're planting, to give our best effort to do things the right way, to make a great product, be respectful to the industry." The winery is young, but already their wines have met with great success. The key, Rick believes, is that "we've been pretty much doing what we said we'd do for 112 years."

ZUCCHINI IN CARPIONE

Chef Jason Stratton of Spinasse gets an abundance of Italian heirloom varieties of zucchini from his friends Jason and Siri at Local Roots Farm. He recommends this summery marinated vegetable antipasti as a great way to use up a lot of zucchini, as it keeps for up to two weeks and improves in flavor. Traditionally a way to preserve fish like sardines or carp (hence the name), you can do the same thing with pounded chicken or turkey breasts.

2 medium zucchini (about 1 pound)

Kosher salt and freshly ground black pepper

Good-quality extra-virgin olive oil, for frying

1 medium yellow onion, cut into ¼-inch dice

3 cloves garlic, sliced

1½ cups white wine (dry, crisp, and drinkable)

2 tablespoons red wine vinegar, plus more to taste

Small handful of mint leaves, roughly chopped

1 bunch Italian parsley, roughly chopped (about 1 packed cup)

Wash and trim the zucchini and then cut them lengthwise into ¼-inch slices. Set the slices out on a clean work surface, sprinkle them with salt, and let them stand for about an hour to draw out excess moisture. Pat the zucchini dry with a clean kitchen towel or paper towels, and season them to taste with pepper.

Add ⅛ inch olive oil to a large frying pan over medium-high heat. Fry the zucchini slices until golden, about 2 minutes, then flip them and lightly cook the other side, about 1 minute. Fry the slices in batches to cook them evenly. Transfer them to a baking sheet or platter to cool.

While the zucchini is cooling, reduce the heat under the pan to medium-low and add the onion. Cook slowly until very soft and starting to turn golden, 12 to 15 minutes, stirring occasionally. Add the garlic and continue cooking until the garlic turns pale golden, another 5 to 7 minutes. Add the wine and vinegar and increase the heat to medium high. Simmer until the liquid has reduced to about the level of the onions, about 10 minutes. Stir in the mint and parsley and taste for salt and acid. The liquid should be well seasoned and rather tart; add more vinegar if needed.

Put a little of the onion mixture in the bottom of a ceramic baking dish or terrine. Alternate layers of zucchini and the onion mixture, making sure each slice is generously coated with onion. After all the slices are in, press down gently with the back of a spoon and cover the top with a thin layer of olive oil. Let cool at room temperature. Store in the refrigerator, but bring to room temperature before serving either by itself, or with crusty artisan bread.

MAKES 4 TO 6 SERVINGS

J. BOOKWALTER WINERY

Making Wine, Literally

When the Washington wine industry was just a fledgling in the 1970s, many of its finest wines (and even some from Oregon) were made with grapes from three of the state's largest plantings of vinifera grapes at Sagemoor Farms, Bacchus, and Dionysus vineyards. In 1975, Jerry Bookwalter moved here from California, where he was growing peaches, almonds, and grapes, to manage these properties, and six months later his wife, Jean, daughter, Terri, and son, John, followed. They lived at the vineyards, twenty miles north of Pasco, for five years before moving into town. Then in 1982, Jerry finally got the winery bug, John says, and he left Sagemoor to try his hand at making wine under his own label. He'd been selling grapes to winemaking pioneers like Rick Small at Woodward Canyon, Gary Figgins at Leonetti Cellars, and S. W. Preston. He'd decided that if they could do it, then he could, too, John explains.

Although Jerry left Sagemoor, he continued to manage other smaller vineyards. He also started a grape brokering business, a property management company, and set up Bookwalter Winery in a warehouse in Pasco. A year later, John graduated from high school and left for college in Tempe, Arizona. Growing up on the family farm in California, doing chores like moving irrigation, working at sorting tables, driving a tractor, and drying grapes for raisins, he swore he'd never farm. And after eight years

living outside Pasco, the teenager was looking for a big city life.

After John left, Bookwalter Winery continued to grow slowly. In 1993 Jerry purchased six acres in the middle of nowhere, just outside Richland, where he made wine and managed vineyards and other properties from his office. Jean ran the tasting room and kept the books; both worked hard and did whatever was necessary. They produced mainly sweet white wines because, as John explains, "It's good for cash flow—you can make a tank in November and bottle it up by January." The couple lived in an apartment on one end of the building, next to the tasting room. The bottle labels showed a pastoral scene of rolling wheat fields with a river running through them.

After Jerry hurt his back in 1995, John discussed with his parents the idea of returning home to help out. John had worked for Gallo Wine Company as a sales representative after college, where he'd become a district manager in Southern California, and was later recruited by a team of former Gallo employees who were producing and selling beverages and a new syrup. The atmosphere there was entrepreneurial, and John loved it. But after a few years, the company faltered, and John went to work for Coors Brewing Company, working his way up to managing their business in the Northwest. He missed the entrepreneurial side of things, so coming home felt like a natural fit. "Here I was in packaged goods sales and management for ten years, working with some of the largest wholesalers and distributors in the United States, working for some of the largest beverage suppliers on earth. So I'd developed a lot of skill sets that would really help out the winery."

First John did a SWOT analysis—presenting the winery's strengths, weaknesses, opportunities, and threats to his parents. John jokes that he knew before his analysis that there was a lot of work to do, "But I didn't know it needed a defibrillator!" His parents moved out of the little apartment on the premises, and John and his girlfriend, Gretchen (now his wife), moved in. "One of my primary objectives was definitely to help my parents, but also I thought that this could be my platform to really build something."

"We had to reinvent ourselves," he says. "There's not been a stone left unturned. My parents were real partners in that, but it also came with a lot of trials and tribulations and challenges." They changed the name to J. Bookwalter, redesigned the label, went from producing primarily sweet white wine to more elegant but flavorful and full-bodied red wines, with just a few whites. They source grapes from some of the top vineyards in the state, including vineyards Jerry still manages.

Despite the fact that Jerry Bookwalter is the ninth generation of his family to farm, John never imagined that he'd be involved in farming of any kind ever again—yet here he is. "This type of business, it's really fuel for my soul and my mind," he admits. "Here's a business where I can wake up in Eastern Washington and be in the vineyard in the morning, and that evening I can be in the swankiest restaurant in Manhattan entertaining clients, talking about where I was that morning! There are few businesses that allow that range of interests." John

says he's a sales guy at heart, and people are his fuel.

Lucky for John, J. Bookwalter is a very social business even though it's in Richland. Stop by the winery on a Friday or Saturday night, and it's standing room only with live music. J. Bookwalter hasn't moved, but today it's an "urban winery" located one minute from the freeway, surrounded by other wineries and housing developments.

John also appreciates that the business allows him to be incredibly creative. Not only through the wine itself, but "if you think about it," he says, "it's a packaging person's dream!"

John has always used a consultant winemaker, and he gratefully acknowledges that his well-received, luscious J. Bookwalter wines are a collaborative effort. He relies on Michael DeMartinis and Travis Maple (the guys who work in his cellar), and on his current consultant winemaker Claude Gros, to help him grow and learn as a winemaker. He gained valuable knowledge and experience working with his former consultant, Zelma Long, and his father's incredible experience growing grapes leaves an indelible mark on the wines as well.

John and Gretchen have two young daughters, and he believes they can do what they want with their lives, as long as they're passionate about it. "Maybe they'll be winemakers or want to go dig ditches or save lives. Whatever, as long as they have fun." Business always interested John; he knows he's lucky he found his parents' interesting. "I always thought, what if my Dad had had a plumbing parts store out here, all elbows and galvanized pipe. I can honestly say that I doubt I'd be back. It wouldn't have served me well. I wouldn't have served it well." Fortunately, he's always loved the beverage industry. "It's a blast to be in. You're selling

good times in many ways. And in this particular business you're selling a lot more—where it's grown and how it's created."

When John and Zelma were working on a new wine in 2004, he decided to use the company name in a new way, making the most of the "book" in Bookwalter. Because it was the first high-end blend they'd produced (made from the fabulous 2002 vintage), he named it Chapter 1. It was released in early 2005 to stellar reviews. To reserve the name for top vintages, he didn't make one the next couple of years—and customers laughingly asked if he had writer's block. That gave him the idea to use literary terms for the whole brand—if he chose carefully, he could say a lot about each wine just through its name. Protagonist (the central hero) is the merlot-based blend that showcases the classic flavors of Washington merlot. Conflict is also a merlot-based blend, but it represents a very different flavor profile less common to Washington merlots. Foreshadow wines are high end but don't come from Chapter vintages, and Subplots are less expensive and more approachable, yet still represent the flavor profile John aims for throughout the brand. Inspired by his literary associations, and by his daughters, John has partnered the winery with a number of literacy-related philanthropies to whom they donate wine and proceeds.

In addition to making wine and running the business of the winery, John is also chairman of the Washington Wine Commission and of the Tri-Cities Visitor and Convention Bureau. Since visitors to wineries account for much of the tourist traffic in Eastern Washington, John's concurrent chairmanships overlap in many ways—what's good for one business is good for the other. His primary role at the Wine Commission is to evangelize Washington wine, particularly appropriate given that his father grew wine grapes back when there weren't even enough Washington wineries to buy them all, and it was almost impossible to sell Washington wine outside the state. Since then the industry has grown and become much more sophisticated, and so has J. Bookwalter.

BLACKBERRY SORBET
WITH CABERNET SAUVIGNON

Pastry Chef Brittany Bardeleben churns this rich, creamy sorbet for Seattle restaurants Crow and Betty. Brittany explains, "Northwest native Cascade blackberries, or 'trailing' blackberries are smaller and more flavorful than the giant Himalayan blackberries typically found in grocery stores. Look for these in the late summer months at farmers markets. I bulked up on Cascade blackberries this year and froze them so I could make this dessert in the dead of winter." If using frozen berries, she says, just let them thaw before making the sorbet.

1 pound blackberries (about 4 cups), preferably Cascades

1 cup water

½ cup plus 2 tablespoons Washington cabernet sauvignon

2 cups simple syrup*

Fresh lemon juice

In a medium pot, combine the blackberries, water, and ½ cup of the wine; bring to a full boil over medium-high heat. Reduce the heat to medium-low and let simmer, covered, for 10 minutes. Remove from the heat, take off the lid, and stir to break up the berries. Allow the mixture to cool for 30 minutes.

Using a blender, purée the cooled, cooked berries in several batches. Press the purée through a fine sieve to remove the seeds. You should have about 2 cups of thick blackberry purée. Add the simple syrup and the remaining 2 tablespoons wine. Taste the sorbet base and add a teaspoon of lemon juice if you'd like. Refrigerate the sorbet base until it is thoroughly chilled (the colder the base, the faster it will freeze—and that will prevent an overly fluffy and pale-colored finished product). Churn in an ice cream maker according to the manufacturer's instructions.

* Simple syrup can be found in bar supply stores, but it's easier and cheaper to make your own. Combine 2 cups water and 2 cups sugar in a medium pot. Bring to a full boil over high heat, boil for just a few seconds, then let it cool completely. Store any leftover simple syrup in the refrigerator for cocktails or for sweetening iced tea.

MAKES ABOUT 1 QUART SORBET

APPENDIX I:
Where to Find the Producers

Alm Hill Gardens

Products available at farmers markets in Seattle, Bellevue, Fairhaven, and Bellingham; CSA boxes are offered June–October through the Growing Whatcom collaborative CSA. More information available at www.growingwashington.org.

Alvarez Farms

"Fresh Organic Produce Grown in the Yakima Valley"

Products available at 14 farmers markets all over Seattle, as well as in Yakima, Pasco, Puyallup, Kirkland, Kent, and Renton.

Billy's Gardens

"Grown in the Northwest for People in the Northwest"

Products available at 11 farmers markets in the Seattle area including Federal Way, Queen Anne, Georgetown, and Bellevue. Billy's produce can also be found at Whole Foods markets in 6 locations around Seattle. For a complete list, visit www.billys gardens.com.

Bluebird Grain Farms

"Organic Heirloom Grains from Plow to Package"

Often at the University District farmers market and always available at a number of retail locations throughout the state. Products are also available through their CSA program and online ordering. Visit www.bluebirdgrainfarms.com/retail-locations.html.

Booth Canyon Orchard

"Certified Organic Heirloom Fruit"

Available at the University District and West Seattle farmers markets, through the Bainbridge Island CSA, on Vashon Island, and in the Methow Valley. Visit www.booth canyonorchard.com for a complete list.

Cadaretta Wines

Available at a number of fine restaurants and wine shops, or from their website at www.cadaretta.com.

J. Bookwalter Winery

"Literally, the Best of Washington Wine"

Available at a number of fine restaurants and wine shops, at the winery and tasting room in Richland, at the tasting studio in Woodinville, or from their website at www.bookwalter wines.com.

Kurtwood Farms

"Farmstead Cheese"

Available at a number of retailers in the Seattle area and at the Vashon Island Thriftway, and served at a long list of Seattle restaurants. For exact locations, visit www.kurtwood farms.com.

Loki Fish Co.

"Sustainably Harvesting and Direct-Marketing Wild Fish, with Integrity from Sea to Table."

Available in the Seattle area at 8 farmers markets, at many restaurants, directly off the *Njord* at Seattle's Fishermen's Terminal West Wall, from a number of stores listed at www.lokifish.com/product-markets.html, and from their online store at www.lokifish.com.

Olsen Farms

"Specializing in Gourmet Potatoes"

Available year-round at Ballard and University District farmers markets, and seasonally at 9 other market locations. Visit www.olsenfarms.com/where.htm for a complete list of farmers markets and restaurants.

Pelindaba Lavender

Products are available at stores on the Pelindaba farm on San Juan Island, in Friday Harbor, and in Santa Rosa, California, and from their online store at www.pelindaba lavender.com, where maps and directions to the farm are also available.

Pipitone Farms

"Organic Growers Since 1978"

Fresh produce as well as their farm-made line of jarred and bottled products available at farmers markets throughout the Seattle area, including those at the University District and Queen Anne. For more information contact Pipitone Farms at pipitonefarms@msn.com.

Port Madison Goat Farm and Dairy

Cheese and yogurt available at farmers markets throughout the Puget Sound including Bainbridge Island, Ballard, and West Seattle, and at a number of co-ops and specialty stores.

Tahuya River Apiaries

"Bee Products Made the Natural Way"

Available at the University District and Ballard farmers markets, and from their online store at www.hiveharvest.com.

Taylor Shellfish

"Fresh Shellfish from the Pacific Northwest"

Available at their stores at the Samish Bay and Shelton farms, and at their new store location in Capitol Hill (visit www.taylorshellfishfarms.com for directions), from other stores and restaurants throughout the state, or from their online store at www.taylorshellfish store.com.

Turnbow Flat Farm

"All-Natural, Pasture-Based, Grass-Fed"

Available at the farm just outside Palouse, Washington, or by advance order via e-mail or telephone. 509-878-1758. www.turnbowflatfarm.com.

Wild Things

"Choice Edible Mushrooms, Berries, and Weeds"

Available at the University District farmers market in Seattle.

APPENDIX II:
The Restaurants

Barking Frog
14580 NE 145th Street
Woodinville, WA 98072
425-424-2999
www.willowslodge.com

Betty Restaurant & Bar
1507 Queen Anne Avenue N
Seattle, WA 98109
206-352-3773
www.eatatbetty.com

The Black Cypress
215 E Main Street
Pullman, WA 99163
509-334-5800
www.theblackcypress.com

BOKA KITCHEN + BAR
1010 1st Avenue
Seattle, WA 98104
206-357-9000
www.bokaseattle.com

Café Presse
1117 12th Avenue
Seattle, WA 98122
206-709-7674
www.cafepresseseattle.com

Canlis Restaurant
2576 Aurora Avenue N
Seattle, WA 98109
206-283-3313
www.canlis.com

Coastal Kitchen
429 15th Avenue E
Seattle, WA 98112
206-322-1145
www.seattle-eats.com

The Corson Building
5609 Corson Avenue S
Seattle, WA 98108
206-762-3330
www.thecorsonbuilding.com
www.sitkaandspruce.com

Crow Restaurant & Bar
823 5th Avenue N
Seattle, WA 98109
206-283-8800
www.eatatcrow.com

Crush
2319 E Madison Street
Seattle, WA 98112
206-302-7874
www.chefjasonwilson.com

Dahlia Lounge

2001 4th Avenue
Seattle, WA 98121
206-682-4142
www.tomdouglas.com

The Dining Room at Salish Lodge & Spa

6501 Railroad Avenue SE
Snoqualmie, WA 98065
425-888-2556
www.salishlodge.com

Eva Restaurant

2227 N 56th Street
Seattle, WA 98107
206-633-3538
www.evarestaurant.com

The Herbfarm

14590 NE 145th Street
Woodinville, WA 98072
425-485-5300
www.theherbfarm.com

Hudson Public House

8014 15th Avenue NE
Seattle, WA 98115
206-524-5070
www.hudsonpublichouse.com

June

1423 34th Avenue
Seattle, WA 98122
206-323-4000
www.juneseattle.com

Le Pichet

1933 1st Avenue
Seattle, WA 98101
206-256-1499
www.lepichetseattle.com

Chef Robin Leventhal

www.cravefood.com

Lisa Dupar Catering and Pomegranate Bistro

18005 NE 68th Street
Redmond, WA 98052
425-556-5972
www.duparandcompany.com

Macrina Bakery

2408 1st Avenue
Seattle, WA 98121
206-448-4032
www.macrinabakery.com

Marché Bistro and Wine Bar

86 Pine Street
Seattle, WA 98101
206-728-2800
www.marcheseattle.com

Matt's in the Market

94 Pike Street, Suite 32
Seattle, WA 98101
206-467-7909
www.mattsinthemarket.com

Osteria La Spiga

1429 12th Avenue
Seattle, WA 98122
206-323-8881
www.laspiga.com

Parfait

Various "mobile parlor" locations

www.parfait-icecream.com

Picnic

6801 Greenwood Avenue N

Seattle, WA 98103

206-453-5867

www.picnicseattle.com

Poppy

622 Broadway Avenue E

Seattle, WA 98102

206-324-1108

www.poppyseattle.com

Portage Bay Cafe

4130 Roosevelt Way NE

Seattle, WA 98105

206-547-8230

www.portagebaycafe.com

Portals at Suncadia

3600 Suncadia Trail

Cle Elum, WA 98922

866-904-6301

www.suncadiaresort.com

Ravish

2956 Eastlake Avenue E

Seattle, WA 98102

206-913-2497

www.ravishoneastlake.com

Salty's on Alki

1936 Harbor Avenue SW

Seattle, WA 98126

206-937-1600

www.saltys.com

Seastar

205 108th Avenue NE, Suite 100

Bellevue, WA 98004

425-456-0010

www.seastarrestaurant.com

Serafina

2043 Eastlake Avenue E

Seattle, WA 98102

206-323-0807

www.serafinaseattle.com

Spinasse

1531 14th Avenue

Seattle, WA 98122

206-251-7673

www.spinasse.com

Spring Hill

4437 California Avenue SW

Seattle, WA 98116

206-935-1075

www.springhillnorthwest.com

Staple & Fancy Mercantile

4739 Ballard Avenue NW

Seattle, WA 98107

206-789-1200

www.ethanstowellrestaurants.com

Table 219

219 Broadway Avenue E

Seattle, WA 98102

206-328-4604

www.table219.com

TASTE Restaurant

1300 1st Avenue

Seattle, WA 98101

206-903-5291

www.tastesam.com

Tilth

1411 North 45th Street

Seattle, WA 98103

206-633-0801

www.tilthrestaurant.com

Tulio Restaurant

1100 Fifth Avenue

Seattle, WA 98101

206-624-5500

www.tulio.com

Volunteer Park Café

1501 17th Avenue East

Seattle, WA 98112

206-328-3155

www.alwaysfreshgoodness.com

ROCK ISLAND RED

APRICOTS RILAND

~~APRICOTS RILAND~~
PEACHES RED HAVEN   NET WT.

PIPITONE FARMS 5541 PENN AVENUE • ROCK ISLAND, WA 98850

18

#2

24

ATE

U.D.A.
CERTIFIED ORGANIC

S

Fruit

ROCK ISLAND RED

APRICOTS

~~APRICOTS~~ ~~RILAND~~
PEACHES RED HAVEN

Pipitone Farms • 5541 Penn Avenue • Rock Island, WA 98850 • pipitonefarms@msn.com

#2

TATE

PRODUCE OF U.S.A.

TATE

ROCK ISLAND RED

~~PEACHES RED HAVEN~~

APRICOTS RILAND

PIPITONE FARMS 5541 PENN AVE., ROCK ISLAND, WA 98850   NET WT.

2.

S

PRODUCE

INDEX

Note: Photographs are indicated by *italics*.

ABOUT THE AUTHOR

LEORA BLOOM is a freelance writer whose work has been published in the *Seattle Times* and *Seattle* magazine. She trained at Le Cordon Bleu Paris; worked as a pastry chef in Washington, DC, and San Francisco; ran her own bakery in Bellevue, Washington; and tested recipes for a number of cookbooks. She is an avid baker who loves to shop at farmers markets and travel. She lives in Seattle with her husband, three children, and their dog.

About the Photographer

CLARE BARBOZA is a Seattle-based food photographer, with a passion for documenting how food goes from the farm to the kitchen to the table. She has photographed several cookbooks and regularly shoots for various publications, restaurants, and chefs. She also leads a variety of photography workshops out of her studio in downtown Seattle.